THE PYTHON
CODE WARRIOR

Doing ADO with Gusto!

By Richard Thomas Edwards

CONTENTS

Working With ADO
Let's make working with ADO easy

The hardest part of working with ADO looking for
help on the web and none of it makes sense.
—Richard Thomas Edwards

ave you found this to be true: You go up to the web, type in a couple of key words and a whole lot of "not even close" results popup. Even the ones that look promising, are a piece of the whole puzzle and doesn't make it easy for you to compare what you may have been able to do already with what you need to do next. Well you've come to the right place to get the steps down and help you make your Python experience with ADO a pleasure instead of a pain and a frustrating run around.

There are four principle parts to working with ADO.

1. The connection must be made to a local or remote database that is either physical or is running as a service.
2. The version of a physical database must be known.
3. You must determine whether the database requires a username or password to connect to it.
4. You need to know the name of the table you want to use to return data from.

Yes, it can get much more complex than that. You may have to create some complex queries. Things like joins and stored procedures may be on your radar but right now, let's just get you connected.

The first object you want to create is the ADODB.Connection. There is also something that will help you make it visually easier to do all of this. This is what you do:

```
import win32com.client

cn = win32com.client.Dispatch("ADODB.Connection")
dl = win32com.client.Dispatch("DataLinks")
cn = dl.PromptNew()
print cn.connectionstring
```

Copy the code from here, open notepad and save the file as "Datakinks.py" – yes, the quotes are required. Then run it by clicking on the icon that got produced as a Python file.

This code will produce this:

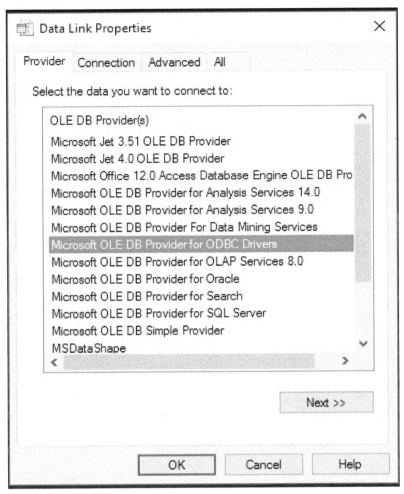

Let's suppose I know I want to connect to an older database. One with a .mdb extension. If I click on the Microsoft.Jet.OLEDB.4.0 and then click on the connection tab and then click on the search button:

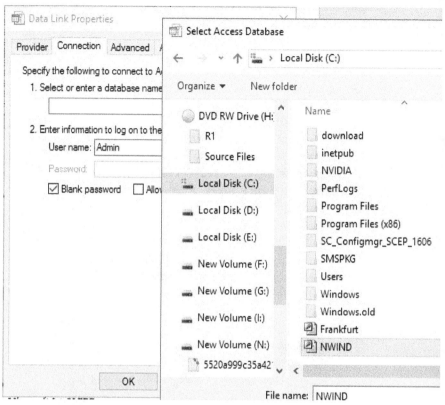

I am ten able to look for the file, click okay and:

Now, I'm ready to test the connection. And when I click on Test connection:

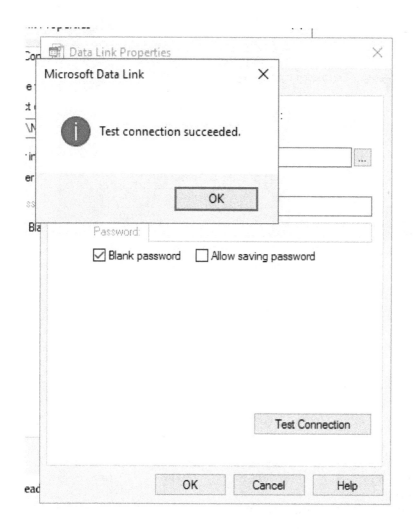

And when you close this all down, your connection string would be:

Provider=Microsoft.Jet.OLEDB.4.0;Data Source=C:\NWIND.MDB;Persist Security Info=False

What about if you already have a connection String and want to test it

import win32com.client

```
cn = win32com.client.Dispatch("ADODB.Connection")
cn.Provider="Microsoft.Jet.OLEDB.4.0"
```

```
cn.Properties("Data Source").Value = "C:\\NWIND.MDB"
dl = win32com.client.Dispatch("DataLinks")
dl.PromptEdit(cn)
print(cn.connectionstring)
```

After you've cleared the semi-colon right after the mdb and when you click on Test Connection.

And it returns:

Provider=Microsoft.Jet.OLEDB.4.0;Data Source="C:\NWIND.MDB;"

HOW CONNECTION STRINGS WORK

So, what is a connection string?

A connection string is a Set of properties you put together on a single line that tells the connection, command or Recordset what provider, driver or ISAM to use and where to look for the database.

Here's pretty much, the classical connection string:

Provider=Microsoft.Jet.OLEDB.4.0;Data Source=C:\NWIND.MDB;Persist Security Info=False

ADO is an acronym for Active-X Data Objects. In VBSCRIPT, you can use it to connect to both the 32-bit and 64-bit versions of Providers, Drivers and ISAMS

The reason why ADO came about in the first place was because DAO relied a lot on disk drives to do most of the work and disk drives were extremely slow.

It is also what was used to build the .Net ODBC, OLEDB, Oracle Client and SQL Client components. So, everything you do in ADO can be applied to the various .Net world as well. Therefore, if you learn ADO, the others are self-explanatory and a walk in the park.

This toolkit includes:

- ADODB.Connection
- ADODB.Command
- ADODB.Recordset

While I love working with SQL Server, I use it in its simplest of terms. I create a connection string cnstr and then a strQuery as my SQL query string.

Here' how these combinations have been worked with in the past:

- Connection, Command and Recordset
- Connection and Recordset
- Command and Recordset
- Recordset

Most of my experiences deal with these four conventions although I have used the ADODB.STREAM with XML and ADSI.

Coding Conventions

Below, are the ways you will find the ADODB.Connection, ADODB.Command and ADODB.Recordset used today. Just remember that they are not scribed in cement and there is more than one way to get the connection to work.

```
import win32com.client
import string
```

Alternative connection one:

```
cn = win32com.client.Dispatch("ADODB.Connection")
cn.Provider="Microsoft.Jet.OLEDB.4.0"
cn.Properties("Data Source").Value = "C:\\NWIND.MDB"
```

Alternative connection two:

```
cn = win32com.client.Dispatch("ADODB.Connection")
cn.Open("Microsoft.Jet.OLEDB.4.0;Data Source = "C:\\NWIND.MDB")
```

Connection, Command and Recordset

```
cn = win32com.client.Dispatch("ADODB.Connection")
cmd = win32com.client.Dispatch("ADODB.Command")
rs = win32com.client.Dispatch("ADODB.Recordset")

cn.ConnectionString = cnstr
cn.Open()

cmd.ActiveConnection = cn
cmd.CommandType=1
cmd.CommandText = "Select * From [Products]"
cmd.Execute()

rs.CursorLocation = 3
rs.LockType = 3
rs.Open(cmd)

rs.MoveFirst()
```

Connection and Recordset

```
cn = win32com.client.Dispatch("ADODB.Connection")
rs = win32com.client.Dispatch("ADODB.Recordset")
cn.ConnectionString = cnstr
cn.Open()

rs.ActiveConnection = cn
rs.CursorLocation = 3
rs.LockType = 3
rs.Open("Select * From [Products]")
```

```
rs.MoveFirst()
```

Command and Recordset

```
cmd = win32com.client.Dispatch("ADODB.Command")
rs = win32com.client.Dispatch("ADODB.Recordset")

cmd.ActiveConnection =  cnstr
cmd.CommandType=1
cmd.CommandText = "Select * From [Products]"
cmd.Execute()

rs.CursorLocation = 3
rs.LockType = 3
rs.Open(cmd)

rs.MoveFirst()
```

Recordset

```
rs = win32com.client.Dispatch("ADODB.Recordset")
rs.ActiveConnection = cnstr
rs.CursorLocation = 3
rs.LockType = 3
rs.Open("Select * From [Products]")

rs.MoveFirst()
```

Tables and Views

At this point you're probably scratching your head trying to figure out how I went from creating a query against a known table. Well aside from the fact that I do know this because I've use that database for lots of examples over the years, I also know that cn.OpenSchema works with the Microsoft.Jet.OleDb.4.0 provider and that the value is 20.

```python
import win32com.client
import string

cn = win32com.client.Dispatch("ADODB.Connection")
rs = win32com.client.Dispatch("ADODB.Recordset")
cn.Provider="Microsoft.Jet.OLEDB.4.0"
cn.Properties("Data Source").Value = "C:\\NWIND.MDB"
cn.Open()

rs = cn.OpenSchema(20)

while rs.EOF == False:
    if str(rs.Fields["TABLE_TYPE"].Value) == "TABLE":
        print(str(rs.Fields["TABLE_NAME"].Value))

    rs.MoveNext()
```

The Results:

Categories

Customers

Employees

Order Details

Orders

Products

Shippers

Suppliers

As for Views:

```
import win32com.client
import string

cn = win32com.client.Dispatch("ADODB.Connection")
rs = win32com.client.Dispatch("ADODB.Recordset")
cn.Provider="Microsoft.Jet.OLEDB.4.0"
cn.Properties("Data Source").Value = "C:\\NWIND.MDB"
cn.Open()

rs = cn.OpenSchema(20)

while rs.EOF == False:
    if str(rs.Fields["TABLE_TYPE"].Value) == "VIEW":
        print(str(rs.Fields["TABLE_NAME"].Value))

    rs.MoveNext()
```

The Results:

Category Sales for 1995
Current Product List
Invoices
Order Details Extended
Order Subtotals
Product Sales for 1995
Products Above Average Price
Quarterly Orders
Sales by Category
Ten Most Expensive Products

A few words of caution here. The Schema types are provider specific, so don't expect the same syntax I just used with the Microsoft.Jet.OLEDB.4.0 provider if you are using the SQL Server or Oracle provider. Not only will the Schema Type be different so will the field names be different, too.

Okay, so now you know something about connection strings and how to get table and view information, it is time to start using that information to create an assortment of user outputs which just might make you and your boss get some warm and fuzzy feelings.

ASP CODE

THERE IS NOTING FANTASIC ABOUT CREATING ASP OR ASPX WEB PAGES. In fact, additional hoops must be jumped - web site where you can cut and paste what you just created from here is one of them. So, with that said, I've added enough bells and whistles into the code structure to make it worth your while.

Here's what is in store for you:

- Report View
  - Horizontal
    - None
    - Button
    - Combobox
    - Div
    - Link
    - Listbox
    - Span
    - Textarea
    - Textbox
  - Vertical
    - None
    - Button
    - Combobox
    - Div
    - Link
    - Listbox

- Span
- Textarea
- Textbox

- Table View
  - Horizontal
    - None
    - Button
    - Combobox
    - Div
    - Link
    - Listbox
    - Span
    - Textarea
    - Textbox
  - Vertical
    - None
    - Button
    - Combobox
    - Div
    - Link
    - Listbox
    - Span
    - Textarea
    - Textbox

```
import win32com.client
import string

ws = win32com.client.Dispatch("WScript.Shell")
fso = win32com.client.Dispatch("Scripting.FileSystemObject")
txtstream = fso.OpenTextFile(ws.CurrentDirectory + "\Products.asp", 2, True, -
2)
txtstream.WriteLine("<html>")
txtstream.WriteLine("<head>")
txtstream.WriteLine("<title>" + Tablename + "</title>")
#Add Stylesheet here
txtstream.WriteLine("<body>")
txtstream.WriteLine("</br>")
```

Horizontal Reports

```
txtstream.WriteLine("<table border=0 cellspacing=3 cellpadding=3>")
txtstream.WriteLine("<%")
txtstream.WriteLine("Response.Write(""<tr>""" + vbcrlf)")
for x = 0 in rs.fields.count:
    txtstream.WriteLine("Response.Write(""<th    style=""   font-family:Calibri,
Sans-Serif;font-size:  12px;color:darkred;"""   align='left'   nowrap='nowrap'>" +
rs.Fields(x).Name + "</th>""" + vbcrlf)")

    txtstream.WriteLine("Response.Write(""</tr>""" + vbcrlf)")

while rs.eof = false:
    txtstream.WriteLine("Response.Write(""<tr>""" + vbcrlf)")
    for x = 0 in rs.fields.count:
```

NONE

```
        txtstream.WriteLine("Response.Write(""<td          style=""font-
family:Calibri,    Sans-Serif;font-size:    12px;color:navy;""    align='left'
nowrap='nowrap'>" + rs.Fields(x).Value + "</td>""" + vbcrlf)")
```

Button

```
        txtstream.WriteLine("Response.Write(""<td          style=""font-
family:Calibri,    Sans-Serif;font-size:    12px;color:navy;""    align='left'
nowrap='true'><button style='width:100%;' value ='" + rs.Fields(x).Value + "'>" +
rs.Fields(x).Value + "</button></td>""" + vbcrlf)")
```

COMBOBOX

```
        txtstream.WriteLine("Response.Write(""<td          style=""font-
family:Calibri,    Sans-Serif;font-size:    12px;color:navy;""    align='left'
nowrap='true'><select><option value = """" + rs.Fields(x).Value + """">" +
rs.Fields(x).Value + "</option></select></td>""" + vbcrlf)")
```

DIV

```
        txtstream.WriteLine("Response.Write(""<td          style=""font-
family:Calibri,    Sans-Serif;font-size:    12px;color:navy;""    align='left'
nowrap='true'><div>" + rs.Fields(x).Value + "</div></td>""" + vbcrlf)")
```

LINK

```
        txtstream.WriteLine("Response.Write(""<td          style=""font-
family:Calibri,    Sans-Serif;font-size:    12px;color:navy;""    align='left'
nowrap='true'><a href='" + rs.Fields(x).Value + "'>" + rs.Fields(x).Value +
"</a></td>""" + vbcrlf)")
```

LISTBOX

```
        txtstream.WriteLine("Response.Write(""<td                style="""font-
family:Calibri,      Sans-Serif;font-size:      12px;color:navy;"""      align='left'
nowrap='true'><select multiple><option value = """ + rs.Fields(x).Value + """>" +
rs.Fields(x).Value + "</option></select></td>""" + vbcrlf)")
```

SPAN

```
        txtstream.WriteLine("Response.Write(""<td                style="""font-
family:Calibri,      Sans-Serif;font-size:      12px;color:navy;"""      align='left'
nowrap='true'><span>" + rs.Fields(x).Value + "</span></td>""" + vbcrlf)")
```

TEXTAREA

```
        txtstream.WriteLine("Response.Write(""<td                style="""font-
family:Calibri,      Sans-Serif;font-size:      12px;color:navy;"""      align='left'
nowrap='true'><textarea>" + rs.Fields(x).Value + "</textarea></td>""" + vbcrlf)")
```

TEXTBOX
```
        txtstream.WriteLine("Response.Write(""<td                style="""font-
family:Calibri,      Sans-Serif;font-size:      12px;color:navy;"""      align='left'
nowrap='true'><input      type=text      value="""      +      rs.Fields(x).Value      +
"""></input></td>""" + vbcrlf)")

        txtstream.WriteLine("Response.Write(""</tr>""" + vbcrlf)")
        rs.MoveNext

    txtstream.WriteLine("%>")
    txtstream.WriteLine("</table>")
    txtstream.WriteLine("</body>")
    txtstream.WriteLine("</html>")
```

txtstream.Close()

Vertical Reports

```
txtstream.WriteLine("<table border=0 cellspacing=3 cellpadding=3>")
txtstream.WriteLine("<%")
for x = 0 in rs.fields.count:
    txtstream.WriteLine("Response.Write(""<tr><th    style=""    font-
family:Calibri,    Sans-Serif;font-size:    12px;color:darkred;""    align='left'
nowrap='nowrap'>" + rs.Fields(x).Name + "</th>""" + vbcrlf)")
    rs.MoveFirst()
    while rs.eof = false:
        txtstream.WriteLine("Response.Write(""<td  style=""font-family:Calibri,
Sans-Serif;font-size:  12px;color:navy;"">" + rs.Fields(x).Value  +  "</td>"""  +
vbcrlf)")
```

NONE

```
        txtstream.WriteLine("Response.Write(""<td  style=""font-family:Calibri,
Sans-Serif;font-size:  12px;color:navy;""  align='left'  nowrap='nowrap'>"  +
rs.Fields(x).Value + "</td>""" + vbcrlf)")
```

Button

```
        txtstream.WriteLine("Response.Write(""<td  style=""font-family:Calibri,
Sans-Serif;font-size:  12px;color:navy;""  align='left'  nowrap='true'><button
style='width:100%;' value ='" + rs.Fields(x).Value + "'>" + rs.Fields(x).Value +
"</button></td>""" + vbcrlf)")
```

Combobox

txtstream.WriteLine("Response.Write(""""<td style=""""font-family:Calibri, Sans-Serif;font-size: 12px;color:navy;"""" align='left' nowrap='true'><select><option value = """""" + rs.Fields(x).Value + """"">" + rs.Fields(x).Value + "</option></select></td>"""" + vbcrlf)")

Div

txtstream.WriteLine("Response.Write(""""<td style=""""font-family:Calibri, Sans-Serif;font-size: 12px;color:navy;"""" align='left' nowrap='true'> " + rs.Fields(x).Value + " </td>"""" + vbcrlf)")

Link

txtstream.WriteLine("Response.Write(""""<td style=""""font-family:Calibri, Sans-Serif;font-size: 12px;color:navy;"""" align='left' nowrap='true'><a href='" + rs.Fields(x).Value + "'>" + rs.Fields(x).Value + "</a></td>"""" + vbcrlf)")

Listbox

txtstream.WriteLine("Response.Write(""""<td style=""""font-family:Calibri, Sans-Serif;font-size: 12px;color:navy;"""" align='left' nowrap='true'><select multiple><option value = """""" + rs.Fields(x).Value + """"">" + rs.Fields(x).Value + "</option></select></td>"""" + vbcrlf)")

Span

txtstream.WriteLine("Response.Write(""""<td style=""""font-family:Calibri, Sans-Serif;font-size: 12px;color:navy;"""" align='left' nowrap='true'>" + rs.Fields(x).Value + "</td>"""" + vbcrlf)")

Textarea

```
txtstream.WriteLine("Response.Write(""<td        style=""font-family:Calibri,
Sans-Serif;font-size: 12px;color:navy;"" align='left' nowrap='true'><textarea>" +
rs.Fields(x).Value + "</textarea></td>"" + vbcrlf)")
```

Textbox

```
    txtstream.WriteLine("Response.Write(""<td  style=""font-family:Calibri,
Sans-Serif;font-size:    12px;color:navy;""    align='left'    nowrap='true'><input
type=text value=""" + rs.Fields(x).Value + """></input></td>"" + vbcrlf)")
        rs.MoveNext

    txtstream.WriteLine("Response.Write(""</tr>"" + vbcrlf)")

txtstream.WriteLine("%>")
txtstream.WriteLine("</table>")
txtstream.WriteLine("</body>")
txtstream.WriteLine("</html>")
txtstream.Close()
```

Horizontal Tables

```
txtstream.WriteLine("<table     style='border:Double;border-width:1px;border-
color:navy;' rules=all frames=both cellpadding=2 cellspacing=2 Width=0>")
txtstream.WriteLine("<%")
txtstream.WriteLine("Response.Write(""<tr>"" + vbcrlf)")
for x = 0 in rs.fields.count:
```

```
        txtstream.WriteLine("Response.Write(""<th    style=""   font-family:Calibri,
Sans-Serif;font-size:  12px;color:darkred;""   align='left'  nowrap='nowrap'>"   +
rs.Fields(x).Name + "</th>""" + vbcrlf)")


     while rs.eof = false:
        txtstream.WriteLine("Response.Write(""<tr>""" + vbcrlf)")
          for x = 0 in rs.fields.count:
```

NONE

```
          txtstream.WriteLine("Response.Write(""<td              style=""font-
family:Calibri,      Sans-Serif;font-size:      12px;color:navy;""       align='left'
nowrap='nowrap'>" + rs.Fields(x).Value + "</td>""" + vbcrlf)")
```

Button

```
          txtstream.WriteLine("Response.Write(""<td              style=""font-
family:Calibri,      Sans-Serif;font-size:      12px;color:navy;""       align='left'
nowrap='true'><button style='width:100%;' value ='" + rs.Fields(x).Value + "'>" +
rs.Fields(x).Value + "</button></td>""" + vbcrlf)")
```

COMBOBOX

```
          txtstream.WriteLine("Response.Write(""<td              style=""font-
family:Calibri,      Sans-Serif;font-size:      12px;color:navy;""       align='left'
nowrap='true'><select><option value  =  """  +  rs.Fields(x).Value  +  """">"  +
rs.Fields(x).Value + "</option></select></td>""" + vbcrlf)")
```

DIV

```
txtstream.WriteLine("Response.Write(""<td          style=""font-
family:Calibri,      Sans-Serif;font-size:      12px;color:navy;""      align='left'
nowrap='true'><div>" + rs.Fields(x).Value + "</div></td>"" + vbcrlf)")
```

LINK

```
txtstream.WriteLine("Response.Write(""<td          style=""font-
family:Calibri,      Sans-Serif;font-size:      12px;color:navy;""      align='left'
nowrap='true'><a  href='"  +  rs.Fields(x).Value  +  "'>"  +  rs.Fields(x).Value  +
"</a></td>"" + vbcrlf)")
```

LISTBOX

```
txtstream.WriteLine("Response.Write(""<td          style=""font-
family:Calibri,      Sans-Serif;font-size:      12px;color:navy;""      align='left'
nowrap='true'><select multiple><option value = """" + rs.Fields(x).Value + """">" +
rs.Fields(x).Value + "</option></select></td>"" + vbcrlf)")
```

SPAN

```
txtstream.WriteLine("Response.Write(""<td          style=""font-
family:Calibri,      Sans-Serif;font-size:      12px;color:navy;""      align='left'
nowrap='true'><span>" + rs.Fields(x).Value + "</span></td>"" + vbcrlf)")
```

TEXTAREA

```
txtstream.WriteLine("Response.Write(""<td          style=""font-
family:Calibri,      Sans-Serif;font-size:      12px;color:navy;""      align='left'
nowrap='true'><textarea>" + rs.Fields(x).Value + "</textarea></td>"" + vbcrlf)")
```

TEXTBOX

```
        txtstream.WriteLine("Response.Write(""<td                style=""font-
family:Calibri,    Sans-Serif;font-size:    12px;color:navy;""    align='left'
nowrap='true'><input    type=text    value="""    +    rs.Fields(x).Value    +
""""></input></td>"" + vbcrlf)")

        txtstream.WriteLine("Response.Write(""</tr>"" + vbcrlf)")
        rs.MoveNext

    txtstream.WriteLine("%>")
    txtstream.WriteLine("</table>")
    txtstream.WriteLine("</body>")
    txtstream.WriteLine("</html>")
    txtstream.Close()
```

Vertical Tables

```
    txtstream.WriteLine("<table    style='border:Double;border-width:1px;border-
color:navy;' rules=all frames=both cellpadding=2 cellspacing=2 Width=0>")

    txtstream.WriteLine("<%")

for x = 0 in rs.fields.count:
        txtstream.WriteLine("Response.Write(""<tr><th        style=""    font-
family:Calibri,    Sans-Serif;font-size:    12px;color:darkred;""    align='left'
nowrap='nowrap'>" + rs.Fields(x).Name + "</th>"" + vbcrlf)")
        rs.MoveFirst()
        while rs.eof == False:
        txtstream.WriteLine("Response.Write(""<td  style=""font-family:Calibri,
Sans-Serif;font-size:  12px;color:navy;"">"  +  rs.Fields(x).Value  +  "</td>""  +
vbcrlf)")
```

NONE

txtstream.WriteLine("Response.Write(""<td style=""font-family:Calibri, Sans-Serif;font-size: 12px;color:navy;"" align='left' nowrap='nowrap'>" + rs.Fields(x).Value + "</td>""" + vbcrlf)")

Button

txtstream.WriteLine("Response.Write(""<td style=""font-family:Calibri, Sans-Serif;font-size: 12px;color:navy;"" align='left' nowrap='true'><button style='width:100%;' value ='" + rs.Fields(x).Value + "'>" + rs.Fields(x).Value + "</button></td>""" + vbcrlf)")

Combobox

txtstream.WriteLine("Response.Write(""<td style=""font-family:Calibri, Sans-Serif;font-size: 12px;color:navy;"" align='left' nowrap='true'><select><option value = """ + rs.Fields(x).Value + """">" + rs.Fields(x).Value + "</option></select></td>""" + vbcrlf)")

Div

txtstream.WriteLine("Response.Write(""<td style=""font-family:Calibri, Sans-Serif;font-size: 12px;color:navy;"" align='left' nowrap='true'> " + rs.Fields(x).Value + " </td>""" + vbcrlf)")

Link

txtstream.WriteLine("Response.Write(""<td style=""font-family:Calibri, Sans-Serif;font-size: 12px;color:navy;"" align='left' nowrap='true'><a href='" + rs.Fields(x).Value + "'>" + rs.Fields(x).Value + "</a></td>""" + vbcrlf)")

Listbox

```
txtstream.WriteLine("Response.Write(""<td        style=""font-family:Calibri,
Sans-Serif;font-size:   12px;color:navy;""   align='left'   nowrap='true'><select
multiple><option value = """ + rs.Fields(x).Value + """>" + rs.Fields(x).Value +
"</option></select></td>""" + vbcrlf)")
```

Span

```
txtstream.WriteLine("Response.Write(""<td  style=""font-family:Calibri,
Sans-Serif;font-size: 12px;color:navy;""  align='left' nowrap='true'><span>" +
rs.Fields(x).Value + "</span></td>""" + vbcrlf)")
```

Textarea

```
txtstream.WriteLine("Response.Write(""<td        style=""font-family:Calibri,
Sans-Serif;font-size: 12px;color:navy;""  align='left' nowrap='true'><textarea>" +
rs.Fields(x).Value + "</textarea></td>""" + vbcrlf)")
```

Textbox

```
txtstream.WriteLine("Response.Write(""<td  style=""font-family:Calibri,
Sans-Serif;font-size:   12px;color:navy;""   align='left'   nowrap='true'><input
type=text value=""" + rs.Fields(x).Value + """></input></td>""" + vbcrlf)")
        rs.MoveNext

    txtstream.WriteLine("Response.Write(""</tr>""" + vbcrlf)")

txtstream.WriteLine("%>")
txtstream.WriteLine("</table>")
txtstream.WriteLine("</body>")
```

```
txtstream.WriteLine("</html>")
txtstream.Close()
```

ASPX Code
Chapter Subtitle

*Chapter Epigraph uses a quote or verse to
introduce the chapter and set the stage.*
—Attribute the quote

T HE FIRST PARAGRAPH STYLE GIVES you nice spacing after the title, as well as the right indents for the first part of your text. Try adding uppercase letters to half of the first line for added styling. For even more stylistic impact, add a Drop Cap from the "Format..." menu in Microsoft Word. We recommend using a line height of three for the drop cap in this template.

You can keep adding these styles to as many chapters as you have. Most of your chapters won't have all of the styles we're using here. Just be sure to only use the styles that have the letter "K" before them; that's how you know they belong to this template and will show up right in your Kindle book.

Lorem ipsum dolor sit amet, consectetur adipiscing elit. Cras ac ligula dictum, elementum mi in, lacinia neque. Ut commodo faucibus tellus, sit amet efficitur magna dictum facilisis. Nam at lectus ac mauris convallis mattis nec at arcu. Praesent dignissim cursus risus at luctus. Maecenas metus nisl, gravida eget justo nec, semper tristique mi. Suspendisse suscipit at ex ut faucibus. Pellentesque ut mi elementum sapien pellentesque ultricies a id diam.

```python
import win32com.client
import string

ws = win32com.client.Dispatch("WScript.Shell")
fso = win32com.client.Dispatch("Scripting.FileSystemObject")
txtstream = fso.OpenTextFile(ws.CurrentDirectory + "\Products.asp", 2, True, -2)

txtstream.WriteLine("<html>")
txtstream.WriteLine("<head>")
txtstream.WriteLine("<title>" + Tablename + "</title>")
#Add Stylesheet here
txtstream.WriteLine("<body>")
txtstream.WriteLine("</br>")
```

Horizontal Reports

```python
txtstream.WriteLine("<table border=0 cellspacing=3 cellpadding=3>")
txtstream.WriteLine("<%")
txtstream.WriteLine("Response.Write(""<tr>""" + vbcrlf)")
for x = 0 in rs.fields.count:
    txtstream.WriteLine("Response.Write(""<th    style=""   font-family:Calibri,
Sans-Serif;font-size: 12px;color:darkred;"""   align='left'   nowrap='nowrap'>"   +
rs.Fields(x).Name + "</th>""" + vbcrlf)")

    txtstream.WriteLine("Response.Write(""</tr>""" + vbcrlf)")

while rs.eof = false:
    txtstream.WriteLine("Response.Write(""<tr>""" + vbcrlf)")
    for x = 0 in rs.fields.count:
```

NONE

```
txtstream.WriteLine("Response.Write(""<td                    style="""font-
family:Calibri,     Sans-Serif;font-size:     12px;color:navy;"""     align='left'
nowrap='nowrap'>" + rs.Fields(x).Value + "</td>""" + vbcrlf)")
```

Button

```
txtstream.WriteLine("Response.Write(""<td                    style="""font-
family:Calibri,     Sans-Serif;font-size:     12px;color:navy;"""     align='left'
nowrap='true'><button style='width:100%;' value ='" + rs.Fields(x).Value + "'>" +
rs.Fields(x).Value + "</button></td>""" + vbcrlf)")
```

COMBOBOX

```
txtstream.WriteLine("Response.Write(""<td                    style="""font-
family:Calibri,     Sans-Serif;font-size:     12px;color:navy;"""     align='left'
nowrap='true'><select><option value = """" + rs.Fields(x).Value + """">" +
rs.Fields(x).Value + "</option></select></td>""" + vbcrlf)")
```

DIV

```
txtstream.WriteLine("Response.Write(""<td                    style="""font-
family:Calibri,     Sans-Serif;font-size:     12px;color:navy;"""     align='left'
nowrap='true'><div>" + rs.Fields(x).Value + "</div></td>""" + vbcrlf)")
```

LINK

```
txtstream.WriteLine("Response.Write(""<td                    style="""font-
family:Calibri,     Sans-Serif;font-size:     12px;color:navy;"""     align='left'
nowrap='true'><a href='" + rs.Fields(x).Value + "'>" + rs.Fields(x).Value +
"</a></td>""" + vbcrlf)")
```

LISTBOX

```
        txtstream.WriteLine("Response.Write(""<td                style="""font-
family:Calibri,    Sans-Serif;font-size:    12px;color:navy;"""    align='left'
nowrap='true'><select multiple><option value = """ + rs.Fields(x).Value + """>" +
rs.Fields(x).Value + "</option></select></td>""" + vbcrlf)")
```

SPAN

```
        txtstream.WriteLine("Response.Write(""<td                style="""font-
family:Calibri,    Sans-Serif;font-size:    12px;color:navy;"""    align='left'
nowrap='true'><span>" + rs.Fields(x).Value + "</span></td>""" + vbcrlf)")
```

TEXTAREA

```
        txtstream.WriteLine("Response.Write(""<td                style="""font-
family:Calibri,    Sans-Serif;font-size:    12px;color:navy;"""    align='left'
nowrap='true'><textarea>" + rs.Fields(x).Value + "</textarea></td>""" + vbcrlf)")
```

TEXTBOX
```
        txtstream.WriteLine("Response.Write(""<td                style="""font-
family:Calibri,    Sans-Serif;font-size:    12px;color:navy;"""    align='left'
nowrap='true'><input    type=text    value="""    +    rs.Fields(x).Value    +
"""></input></td>""" + vbcrlf)")

        txtstream.WriteLine("Response.Write(""</tr>""" + vbcrlf)")
        rs.MoveNext

txtstream.WriteLine("%>")
txtstream.WriteLine("</table>")
txtstream.WriteLine("</body>")
txtstream.WriteLine("</html>")
```

```
txtstream.Close()
```

Vertical Reports

```
txtstream.WriteLine("<table border=0 cellspacing=3 cellpadding=3>")
txtstream.WriteLine("<%")
for x = 0 in rs.fields.count:
    txtstream.WriteLine("Response.Write(""<tr><th        style=""    font-
family:Calibri,    Sans-Serif;font-size:    12px;color:darkred;""    align='left'
nowrap='nowrap'>" + rs.Fields(x).Name + "</th>""" + vbcrlf)")
    rs.MoveFirst()
    while rs.eof = false:
        txtstream.WriteLine("Response.Write(""<td style=""font-family:Calibri,
Sans-Serif;font-size:  12px;color:navy;"">" + rs.Fields(x).Value + "</td>""" +
vbcrlf)")
```

NONE

```
        txtstream.WriteLine("Response.Write(""<td style=""font-family:Calibri,
Sans-Serif;font-size:  12px;color:navy;""    align='left'   nowrap='nowrap'>"  +
rs.Fields(x).Value + "</td>""" + vbcrlf)")
```

Button

```
        txtstream.WriteLine("Response.Write(""<td style=""font-family:Calibri,
Sans-Serif;font-size:  12px;color:navy;""    align='left'   nowrap='true'><button
style='width:100%;' value ='" + rs.Fields(x).Value + "'>" + rs.Fields(x).Value +
"</button></td>""" + vbcrlf)")
```

Combobox

txtstream.WriteLine("Response.Write(""""<td style=""""font-family:Calibri, Sans-Serif;font-size: 12px;color:navy;"""" align='left' nowrap='true'><select><option value = """""" + rs.Fields(x).Value + """"">" + rs.Fields(x).Value + "</option></select></td>"""" + vbcrlf)")

Div

txtstream.WriteLine("Response.Write(""""<td style=""""font-family:Calibri, Sans-Serif;font-size: 12px;color:navy;"""" align='left' nowrap='true'> " + rs.Fields(x).Value + " </td>"""" + vbcrlf)")

Link

txtstream.WriteLine("Response.Write(""""<td style=""""font-family:Calibri, Sans-Serif;font-size: 12px;color:navy;"""" align='left' nowrap='true'><a href='" + rs.Fields(x).Value + "'>" + rs.Fields(x).Value + "</a></td>"""" + vbcrlf)")

Listbox

txtstream.WriteLine("Response.Write(""""<td style=""""font-family:Calibri, Sans-Serif;font-size: 12px;color:navy;"""" align='left' nowrap='true'><select multiple><option value = """""" + rs.Fields(x).Value + """"">" + rs.Fields(x).Value + "</option></select></td>"""" + vbcrlf)")

Span

txtstream.WriteLine("Response.Write(""""<td style=""""font-family:Calibri, Sans-Serif;font-size: 12px;color:navy;"""" align='left' nowrap='true'>" + rs.Fields(x).Value + "</td>"""" + vbcrlf)")

Textarea

```
txtstream.WriteLine("Response.Write(""<td        style=""font-family:Calibri,
Sans-Serif;font-size: 12px;color:navy;"" align='left' nowrap='true'><textarea>" +
rs.Fields(x).Value + "</textarea></td>""" + vbcrlf)")
```

Textbox

```
txtstream.WriteLine("Response.Write(""<td style=""font-family:Calibri,
Sans-Serif;font-size:   12px;color:navy;""    align='left'    nowrap='true'><input
type=text value=""" + rs.Fields(x).Value + """></input></td>""" + vbcrlf)")
        rs.MoveNext

txtstream.WriteLine("Response.Write(""</tr>""" + vbcrlf)")

txtstream.WriteLine("%>")
txtstream.WriteLine("</table>")
txtstream.WriteLine("</body>")
txtstream.WriteLine("</html>")
txtstream.Close()
```

Horizontal Tables

```
txtstream.WriteLine("<table       style='border:Double;border-width:1px;border-
color:navy;' rules=all frames=both cellpadding=2 cellspacing=2 Width=0>")
txtstream.WriteLine("<%")
txtstream.WriteLine("Response.Write(""<tr>""" + vbcrlf)")
for x = 0 in rs.fields.count:
```

txtstream.WriteLine("Response.Write(""<th style="" font-family:Calibri, Sans-Serif;font-size: 12px;color:darkred;"" align='left' nowrap='nowrap'>" + rs.Fields(x).Name + "</th>""" + vbcrlf)")

while rs.eof = false:
  txtstream.WriteLine("Response.Write(""<tr>""" + vbcrlf)")
    for x = 0 in rs.fields.count:

NONE

txtstream.WriteLine("Response.Write(""<td style=""font-family:Calibri, Sans-Serif;font-size: 12px;color:navy;"" align='left' nowrap='nowrap'>" + rs.Fields(x).Value + "</td>""" + vbcrlf)")

Button

txtstream.WriteLine("Response.Write(""<td style=""font-family:Calibri, Sans-Serif;font-size: 12px;color:navy;"" align='left' nowrap='true'><button style='width:100%;' value ='" + rs.Fields(x).Value + "'>" + rs.Fields(x).Value + "</button></td>""" + vbcrlf)")

COMBOBOX

txtstream.WriteLine("Response.Write(""<td style=""font-family:Calibri, Sans-Serif;font-size: 12px;color:navy;"" align='left' nowrap='true'><select><option value = """ + rs.Fields(x).Value + """>" + rs.Fields(x).Value + "</option></select></td>""" + vbcrlf)")

DIV

```
txtstream.WriteLine("Response.Write(""<td          style="""font-
family:Calibri,   Sans-Serif;font-size:   12px;color:navy;"""   align='left'
nowrap='true'><div>" + rs.Fields(x).Value + "</div></td>""" + vbcrlf)")
```

LINK

```
txtstream.WriteLine("Response.Write(""<td          style="""font-
family:Calibri,   Sans-Serif;font-size:   12px;color:navy;"""   align='left'
nowrap='true'><a  href='"  +  rs.Fields(x).Value  +  "'>"  +  rs.Fields(x).Value  +
"</a></td>""" + vbcrlf)")
```

LISTBOX

```
txtstream.WriteLine("Response.Write(""<td          style="""font-
family:Calibri,   Sans-Serif;font-size:   12px;color:navy;"""   align='left'
nowrap='true'><select multiple><option value = """" + rs.Fields(x).Value + """">" +
rs.Fields(x).Value + "</option></select></td>""" + vbcrlf)")
```

SPAN

```
txtstream.WriteLine("Response.Write(""<td          style="""font-
family:Calibri,   Sans-Serif;font-size:   12px;color:navy;"""   align='left'
nowrap='true'><span>" + rs.Fields(x).Value + "</span></td>""" + vbcrlf)")
```

TEXTAREA

```
txtstream.WriteLine("Response.Write(""<td          style="""font-
family:Calibri,   Sans-Serif;font-size:   12px;color:navy;"""   align='left'
nowrap='true'><textarea>" + rs.Fields(x).Value + "</textarea></td>""" + vbcrlf)")
```

TEXTBOX

```
        txtstream.WriteLine("Response.Write(""<td                style=""font-
family:Calibri,    Sans-Serif;font-size:    12px;color:navy;""    align='left'
nowrap='true'><input    type=text    value="""    +    rs.Fields(x).Value    +
"""></input></td>"" + vbcrlf)")

        txtstream.WriteLine("Response.Write(""</tr>"" + vbcrlf)")
        rs.MoveNext

    txtstream.WriteLine("%>")
    txtstream.WriteLine("</table>")
    txtstream.WriteLine("</body>")
    txtstream.WriteLine("</html>")
    txtstream.Close()
```

Vertical Tables

```
    txtstream.WriteLine("<table    style='border:Double;border-width:1px;border-
color:navy;' rules=all frames=both cellpadding=2 cellspacing=2 Width=0>")

    txtstream.WriteLine("<%")

    for x = 0 in rs.fields.count:
        txtstream.WriteLine("Response.Write(""<tr><th        style=""    font-
family:Calibri,    Sans-Serif;font-size:    12px;color:darkred;""    align='left'
nowrap='nowrap'>" + rs.Fields(x).Name + "</th>"" + vbcrlf)")
        rs.MoveFirst()
        while rs.eof == False:
        txtstream.WriteLine("Response.Write(""<td  style=""font-family:Calibri,
Sans-Serif;font-size:  12px;color:navy;"">"  +  rs.Fields(x).Value  +  "</td>""  +
vbcrlf)")
```

NONE

```
txtstream.WriteLine("Response.Write(""<td style=""font-family:Calibri,
Sans-Serif;font-size:  12px;color:navy;""  align='left'  nowrap='nowrap'>" +
rs.Fields(x).Value + "</td>"" + vbcrlf)")
```

Button

```
txtstream.WriteLine("Response.Write(""<td style=""font-family:Calibri,
Sans-Serif;font-size:  12px;color:navy;""  align='left'  nowrap='true'><button
style='width:100%;' value ='" + rs.Fields(x).Value + "'>" + rs.Fields(x).Value +
"</button></td>"" + vbcrlf)")
```

Combobox

```
txtstream.WriteLine("Response.Write(""<td style=""font-family:Calibri,
Sans-Serif;font-size: 12px;color:navy;"" align='left' nowrap='true'><select><option
value  =  """  +  rs.Fields(x).Value  +  """">"  +  rs.Fields(x).Value  +
"</option></select></td>"" + vbcrlf)")
```

Div

```
txtstream.WriteLine("Response.Write(""<td        style=""font-family:Calibri,
Sans-Serif;font-size:  12px;color:navy;""  align='left'  nowrap='true'><div>"  +
rs.Fields(x).Value + "</div></td>"" + vbcrlf)")
```

Link

```
txtstream.WriteLine("Response.Write(""<td        style=""font-family:Calibri,
Sans-Serif;font-size: 12px;color:navy;"" align='left' nowrap='true'><a href='" +
rs.Fields(x).Value + "'>" + rs.Fields(x).Value + "</a></td>"" + vbcrlf)")
```

Listbox

```
txtstream.WriteLine("Response.Write(""<td        style=""font-family:Calibri,
Sans-Serif;font-size:    12px;color:navy;""    align='left'    nowrap='true'><select
multiple><option value = """ + rs.Fields(x).Value + """>" + rs.Fields(x).Value +
"</option></select></td>"" + vbcrlf)")
```

Span

```
txtstream.WriteLine("Response.Write(""<td   style=""font-family:Calibri,
Sans-Serif;font-size: 12px;color:navy;""  align='left'  nowrap='true'><span>" +
rs.Fields(x).Value + "</span></td>"" + vbcrlf)")
```

Textarea

```
txtstream.WriteLine("Response.Write(""<td        style=""font-family:Calibri,
Sans-Serif;font-size: 12px;color:navy;""  align='left'  nowrap='true'><textarea>" +
rs.Fields(x).Value + "</textarea></td>"" + vbcrlf)")
```

Textbox

```
txtstream.WriteLine("Response.Write(""<td   style=""font-family:Calibri,
Sans-Serif;font-size:    12px;color:navy;""    align='left'    nowrap='true'><input
type=text value=""" + rs.Fields(x).Value + """></input></td>"" + vbcrlf)")
        rs.MoveNext

    txtstream.WriteLine("Response.Write(""</tr>"" + vbcrlf)")

txtstream.WriteLine("%>")
txtstream.WriteLine("</table>")
txtstream.WriteLine("</body>")
```

```
txtstream.WriteLine("</html>")
txtstream.Close()
```

HTA Code
Chapter Subtitle

Chapter Epigraph uses a quote or verse to
introduce the chapter and set the stage.
—Attribute the quote

IKE ASP AND ASPX, HTA BEEN AROUND FOR SOME TIME NOW. Despite the fact the concept appears to be old or outdated You should know that it is still being used as HTML as an EXE.

```
ws = win32com.client.Dispatch("WScript.Shell")
fso = win32com.client.Dispatch("Scripting.FileSystemObject")
txtstream = fso.OpenTextFile(ws.CurrentDirectory + "\Products.hta", 2, True, -
2)
txtstream.WriteLine("<html>")
txtstream.WriteLine("<head>")
txtstream.WriteLine("<HTA:APPLICATION ")
txtstream.WriteLine("ID = ""Products"" ")
txtstream.WriteLine("APPLICATIONNAME = ""Products"" ")
txtstream.WriteLine("SCROLL = ""yes"" ")
```

```
txtstream.WriteLine("SINGLEINSTANCE = """yes""" ")
txtstream.WriteLine("WINDOWSTATE = """maximize""" >")
txtstream.WriteLine("<title>" + Tablename + "</title>")
#Add Stylesheet here
txtstream.WriteLine("<body>")
txtstream.WriteLine("</br>")
```

Horizontal Reports

```
txtstream.WriteLine("<table border=0 cellspacing=3 cellpadding=3>")
txtstream.WriteLine("<tr>")
for x = 0 in rs.fields.count:
    txtstream.WriteLine("<th style="" font-family:Calibri, Sans-Serif;font-size:
12px;color:darkred;"" align='left' nowrap='nowrap'>" + rs.Fields(x).Name +
"</th>")

    txtstream.WriteLine("</tr>")

    while rs.eof = false:
        txtstream.WriteLine("<tr>")
        for x = 0 in rs.fields.count:
```

NONE

```
        txtstream.WriteLine("<td style="""font-family:Calibri, Sans-Serif;font-
size: 12px;color:navy;"" align='left' nowrap='nowrap'>" + rs.Fields(x).Value +
"</td>")
```

Button

txtstream.WriteLine("<td style="""font-family:Calibri, Sans-Serif;font-size: 12px;color:navy;""" align='left' nowrap='true'><button style='width:100%;' value ='" + rs.Fields(x).Value + "'>" + rs.Fields(x).Value + "</button></td>")

COMBOBOX

txtstream.WriteLine("<td style="""font-family:Calibri, Sans-Serif;font-size: 12px;color:navy;""" align='left' nowrap='true'><select><option value = """ + rs.Fields(x).Value + """>" + rs.Fields(x).Value + "</option></select></td>")

DIV

txtstream.WriteLine("<td style="""font-family:Calibri, Sans-Serif;font-size: 12px;color:navy;""" align='left' nowrap='true'> " + rs.Fields(x).Value + " </td>")

LINK

txtstream.WriteLine("<td style="""font-family:Calibri, Sans-Serif;font-size: 12px;color:navy;""" align='left' nowrap='true'><a href='" + rs.Fields(x).Value + "'>" + rs.Fields(x).Value + "</a></td>")

LISTBOX

txtstream.WriteLine("<td style="""font-family:Calibri, Sans-Serif;font-size: 12px;color:navy;""" align='left' nowrap='true'><select multiple><option value = """ + rs.Fields(x).Value + """>" + rs.Fields(x).Value + "</option></select></td>")

SPAN

txtstream.WriteLine("<td style="""font-family:Calibri, Sans-Serif;font-size: 12px;color:navy;""" align='left' nowrap='true'>" + rs.Fields(x).Value + "</td>")

TEXTAREA

```
txtstream.WriteLine("<td style=""font-family:Calibri, Sans-Serif;font-size: 12px;color:navy;"" align='left' nowrap='true'><textarea>" + rs.Fields(x).Value + "</textarea></td>")
```

TEXTBOX

```
txtstream.WriteLine("<td style=""font-family:Calibri, Sans-Serif;font-size: 12px;color:navy;"" align='left' nowrap='true'><input type=text value=""" + rs.Fields(x).Value + """></input></td>")

txtstream.WriteLine("</tr>")
rs.MoveNext

txtstream.WriteLine("</table>")
txtstream.WriteLine("</body>")
txtstream.WriteLine("</html>")
txtstream.Close()
```

Vertical Reports

```
txtstream.WriteLine("<table border=0 cellspacing=3 cellpadding=3>")
for x = 0 in rs.fields.count:
    txtstream.WriteLine("<tr><th style="" font-family:Calibri, Sans-Serif;font-size: 12px;color:darkred;"" align='left' nowrap='nowrap'>" + rs.Fields(x).Name + "</th>")
    rs.MoveFirst()
    while rs.eof = false:
```

txtstream.WriteLine("<td style=""font-family:Calibri, Sans-Serif;font-size: 12px;color:navy;"">" + rs.Fields(x).Value + "</td>")

NONE

txtstream.WriteLine("<td style=""font-family:Calibri, Sans-Serif;font-size: 12px;color:navy;"" align='left' nowrap='nowrap'>" + rs.Fields(x).Value + "</td>")

Button

txtstream.WriteLine("<td style=""font-family:Calibri, Sans-Serif;font-size: 12px;color:navy;"" align='left' nowrap='true'><button style='width:100%;' value ='" + rs.Fields(x).Value + "'>" + rs.Fields(x).Value + "</button></td>")

Combobox

txtstream.WriteLine("<td style=""font-family:Calibri, Sans-Serif;font-size: 12px;color:navy;"" align='left' nowrap='true'><select><option value = """ + rs.Fields(x).Value + """>" + rs.Fields(x).Value + "</option></select></td>")

Div

txtstream.WriteLine("<td style=""font-family:Calibri, Sans-Serif;font-size: 12px;color:navy;"" align='left' nowrap='true'> " + rs.Fields(x).Value + " </td>")

Link

```
txtstream.WriteLine("<td style=""font-family:Calibri, Sans-Serif;font-size:
12px;color:navy;"" align='left' nowrap='true'><a href='" + rs.Fields(x).Value + "'>"
+ rs.Fields(x).Value + "</a></td>")
```

Listbox

```
txtstream.WriteLine("<td style=""font-family:Calibri, Sans-Serif;font-size:
12px;color:navy;"" align='left' nowrap='true'><select multiple><option value = """
+ rs.Fields(x).Value + """>" + rs.Fields(x).Value + "</option></select></td>")
```

Span

```
txtstream.WriteLine("<td style=""font-family:Calibri, Sans-Serif;font-
size: 12px;color:navy;"" align='left' nowrap='true'><span>" + rs.Fields(x).Value
+ "</span></td>")
```

Textarea

```
txtstream.WriteLine("<td style=""font-family:Calibri, Sans-Serif;font-size:
12px;color:navy;"" align='left' nowrap='true'><textarea>" + rs.Fields(x).Value +
"</textarea></td>")
```

Textbox

```
txtstream.WriteLine("<td style=""font-family:Calibri, Sans-Serif;font-
size: 12px;color:navy;"" align='left' nowrap='true'><input type=text value="""" +
rs.Fields(x).Value + """></input></td>")
        rs.MoveNext

txtstream.WriteLine("</tr>")

txtstream.WriteLine("</table>")
```

```
txtstream.WriteLine("</body>")
txtstream.WriteLine("</html>")
txtstream.Close()
```

Horizontal Tables

```
txtstream.WriteLine("<table     style='border:Double;border-width:1px;border-
color:navy;' rules=all frames=both cellpadding=2 cellspacing=2 Width=0>")
txtstream.WriteLine("<tr>")
for x = 0 in rs.fields.count:
    txtstream.WriteLine("<th style="" font-family:Calibri, Sans-Serif;font-size:
12px;color:darkred;"" align='left' nowrap='nowrap'>" + rs.Fields(x).Name +
"</th>")



while rs.eof = false:
    txtstream.WriteLine("<tr>")
    for x = 0 in rs.fields.count:
```

NONE

```
        txtstream.WriteLine("<td style=""font-family:Calibri, Sans-Serif;font-
size: 12px;color:navy;"" align='left' nowrap='nowrap'>" + rs.Fields(x).Value +
"</td>")
```

Button

txtstream.WriteLine("<td style=""font-family:Calibri, Sans-Serif;font-size: 12px;color:navy;"" align='left' nowrap='true'><button style='width:100%;' value ='" + rs.Fields(x).Value + "'>" + rs.Fields(x).Value + "</button></td>")

COMBOBOX

txtstream.WriteLine("<td style=""font-family:Calibri, Sans-Serif;font-size: 12px;color:navy;"" align='left' nowrap='true'><select><option value = """ + rs.Fields(x).Value + """>" + rs.Fields(x).Value + "</option></select></td>")

DIV

txtstream.WriteLine("<td style=""font-family:Calibri, Sans-Serif;font-size: 12px;color:navy;"" align='left' nowrap='true'> " + rs.Fields(x).Value + " </td>")

LINK

txtstream.WriteLine("<td style=""font-family:Calibri, Sans-Serif;font-size: 12px;color:navy;"" align='left' nowrap='true'><a href='" + rs.Fields(x).Value + "'>" + rs.Fields(x).Value + "</a></td>")

LISTBOX

txtstream.WriteLine("<td style=""font-family:Calibri, Sans-Serif;font-size: 12px;color:navy;"" align='left' nowrap='true'><select multiple><option value = """ + rs.Fields(x).Value + """>" + rs.Fields(x).Value + "</option></select></td>")

SPAN

txtstream.WriteLine("<td style=""font-family:Calibri, Sans-Serif;font-size: 12px;color:navy;"" align='left' nowrap='true'>" + rs.Fields(x).Value + "</td>")

TEXTAREA

txtstream.WriteLine("<td style=""font-family:Calibri, Sans-Serif;font-size: 12px;color:navy;"" align='left' nowrap='true'><textarea>" + rs.Fields(x).Value + "</textarea></td>")

TEXTBOX

txtstream.WriteLine("<td style=""font-family:Calibri, Sans-Serif;font-size: 12px;color:navy;"" align='left' nowrap='true'><input type=text value=""" + rs.Fields(x).Value + """></input></td>")

txtstream.WriteLine("</tr>")
rs.MoveNext

txtstream.WriteLine("</table>")
txtstream.WriteLine("</body>")
txtstream.WriteLine("</html>")
txtstream.Close()

Vertical Tables

txtstream.WriteLine("<table style='border:Double;border-width:1px;border-color:navy;' rules=all frames=both cellpadding=2 cellspacing=2 Width=0>")
for x = 0 in rs.fields.count:
txtstream.WriteLine("<tr><th style="" font-family:Calibri, Sans-Serif;font-size: 12px;color:darkred;"" align='left' nowrap='nowrap'>" + rs.Fields(x).Name + "</th>")
rs.MoveFirst()
while rs.eof == False:

txtstream.WriteLine("<td style="""font-family:Calibri, Sans-Serif;font-size: 12px;color:navy;""">" + rs.Fields(x).Value + "</td>")

NONE

txtstream.WriteLine("<td style="""font-family:Calibri, Sans-Serif;font-size: 12px;color:navy;""" align='left' nowrap='nowrap'>" + rs.Fields(x).Value + "</td>")

Button

txtstream.WriteLine("<td style="""font-family:Calibri, Sans-Serif;font-size: 12px;color:navy;""" align='left' nowrap='true'><button style='width:100%;' value ='" + rs.Fields(x).Value + "'>" + rs.Fields(x).Value + "</button></td>")

Combobox

txtstream.WriteLine("<td style="""font-family:Calibri, Sans-Serif;font-size: 12px;color:navy;""" align='left' nowrap='true'><select><option value = """ + rs.Fields(x).Value + """>" + rs.Fields(x).Value + "</option></select></td>")

Div

txtstream.WriteLine("<td style="""font-family:Calibri, Sans-Serif;font-size: 12px;color:navy;""" align='left' nowrap='true'> " + rs.Fields(x).Value + " </td>")

Link

```
txtstream.WriteLine("<td style=""font-family:Calibri, Sans-Serif;font-size:
12px;color:navy;"" align='left' nowrap='true'><a href='" + rs.Fields(x).Value + "'>"
+ rs.Fields(x).Value + "</a></td>")
```

Listbox

```
txtstream.WriteLine("<td style=""font-family:Calibri, Sans-Serif;font-size:
12px;color:navy;"" align='left' nowrap='true'><select multiple><option value = """
+ rs.Fields(x).Value + """>" + rs.Fields(x).Value + "</option></select></td>")
```

Span

```
txtstream.WriteLine("<td style=""font-family:Calibri, Sans-Serif;font-
size: 12px;color:navy;"" align='left' nowrap='true'><span>" + rs.Fields(x).Value
+ "</span></td>")
```

Textarea

```
txtstream.WriteLine("<td style=""font-family:Calibri, Sans-Serif;font-size:
12px;color:navy;"" align='left' nowrap='true'><textarea>" + rs.Fields(x).Value +
"</textarea></td>")
```

Textbox

```
txtstream.WriteLine("<td style=""font-family:Calibri, Sans-Serif;font-
size: 12px;color:navy;"" align='left' nowrap='true'><input type=text value="""" +
rs.Fields(x).Value + """></input></td>")
        rs.MoveNext

txtstream.WriteLine("</tr>")

txtstream.WriteLine("</table>")
```

```
txtstream.WriteLine("</body>")
txtstream.WriteLine("</html>")
txtstream.Close()
```

HTML CODE

WHAT CAN I SAY ABOUT HTML5 AND CSS THAT HASN'T BEEN SAID ALREADY? Well, I can say that it has come a long way since the 1990s.

```python
import win32com.client
import string

ws = win32com.client.Dispatch("WScript.Shell")
fso = win32com.client.Dispatch("Scripting.FileSystemObject")
txtstream = fso.OpenTextFile(ws.CurrentDirectory + "\Products.html", 2,
True, -2)
txtstream.WriteLine("<html>")
txtstream.WriteLine("<head>")
txtstream.WriteLine("<title>" + Tablename + "</title>")
#Add Stylesheet here
txtstream.WriteLine("<body>")
txtstream.WriteLine("</br>")
```

Horizontal Reports

```python
txtstream.WriteLine("<table border=0 cellspacing=3 cellpadding=3>")
```

```
txtstream.WriteLine("<tr>")
for x = 0 in rs.fields.count:
    txtstream.WriteLine("<th style="" font-family:Calibri, Sans-Serif;font-size:
12px;color:darkred;""  align='left'  nowrap='nowrap'>" +  rs.Fields(x).Name  +
"</th>")

txtstream.WriteLine("</tr>")

while rs.eof = false:
    txtstream.WriteLine("<tr>")
    for x = 0 in rs.fields.count:
```

NONE

```
        txtstream.WriteLine("<td  style=""font-family:Calibri, Sans-Serif;font-
size: 12px;color:navy;""  align='left'  nowrap='nowrap'>" + rs.Fields(x).Value  +
"</td>")
```

Button

```
        txtstream.WriteLine("<td  style=""font-family:Calibri, Sans-Serif;font-
size: 12px;color:navy;""  align='left'  nowrap='true'><button  style='width:100%;'
value ='" + rs.Fields(x).Value + "'>" + rs.Fields(x).Value + "</button></td>")
```

COMBOBOX

```
        txtstream.WriteLine("<td  style=""font-family:Calibri, Sans-Serif;font-
size: 12px;color:navy;""  align='left'  nowrap='true'><select><option value = """ +
rs.Fields(x).Value + """>" + rs.Fields(x).Value + "</option></select></td>")
```

DIV

```
txtstream.WriteLine("<td style=""font-family:Calibri, Sans-Serif;font-
size: 12px;color:navy;"" align='left' nowrap='true'><div>" + rs.Fields(x).Value +
"</div></td>")
```

LINK

```
txtstream.WriteLine("<td style=""font-family:Calibri, Sans-Serif;font-
size: 12px;color:navy;"" align='left' nowrap='true'><a href='" + rs.Fields(x).Value +
"'>" + rs.Fields(x).Value + "</a></td>")
```

LISTBOX

```
txtstream.WriteLine("<td style=""font-family:Calibri, Sans-Serif;font-
size: 12px;color:navy;"" align='left' nowrap='true'><select multiple><option value =
"""" + rs.Fields(x).Value + """">" + rs.Fields(x).Value + "</option></select></td>")
```

SPAN

```
txtstream.WriteLine("<td style=""font-family:Calibri, Sans-Serif;font-
size: 12px;color:navy;"" align='left' nowrap='true'><span>" + rs.Fields(x).Value +
"</span></td>")
```

TEXTAREA

```
txtstream.WriteLine("<td style=""font-family:Calibri, Sans-Serif;font-
size: 12px;color:navy;"" align='left' nowrap='true'><textarea>" + rs.Fields(x).Value
+ "</textarea></td>")
```

TEXTBOX

```
        txtstream.WriteLine("<td style=""""font-family:Calibri, Sans-Serif;font-
size: 12px;color:navy;""" align='left' nowrap='true'><input type=text value=""""" +
rs.Fields(x).Value + """"></input></td>")

        txtstream.WriteLine("</tr>")
        rs.MoveNext

    txtstream.WriteLine("</table>")
    txtstream.WriteLine("</body>")
    txtstream.WriteLine("</html>")
    txtstream.Close()
```

Vertical Reports

```
    txtstream.WriteLine("<table border=0 cellspacing=3 cellpadding=3>")
    for x = 0 in rs.fields.count:
        txtstream.WriteLine("<tr><th    style=""    font-family:Calibri,    Sans-
Serif;font-size:    12px;color:darkred;"""    align='left'    nowrap='nowrap'>"    +
rs.Fields(x).Name + "</th>")
        rs.MoveFirst()
        while rs.eof = false:
            txtstream.WriteLine("<td style=""""font-family:Calibri, Sans-Serif;font-
size: 12px;color:navy;"""">" + rs.Fields(x).Value + "</td>")
```

NONE

```
        txtstream.WriteLine("<td    style=""""font-family:Calibri,    Sans-Serif;font-
size:    12px;color:navy;""" align='left' nowrap='nowrap'>" + rs.Fields(x).Value +
"</td>")
```

Button

```
        txtstream.WriteLine("<td  style=""font-family:Calibri, Sans-Serif;font-
size:  12px;color:navy;""  align='left'  nowrap='true'><button  style='width:100%;'
value ='" + rs.Fields(x).Value + "'>" + rs.Fields(x).Value + "</button></td>")
```

Combobox

```
        txtstream.WriteLine("<td  style=""font-family:Calibri, Sans-Serif;font-
size:  12px;color:navy;""  align='left'  nowrap='true'><select><option value = """ +
rs.Fields(x).Value + """>" + rs.Fields(x).Value + "</option></select></td>")
```

Div

```
        txtstream.WriteLine("<td  style=""font-family:Calibri, Sans-Serif;font-size:
12px;color:navy;""   align='left'   nowrap='true'><div>"   +   rs.Fields(x).Value   +
"</div></td>")
```

Link

```
        txtstream.WriteLine("<td  style=""font-family:Calibri, Sans-Serif;font-size:
12px;color:navy;""  align='left'  nowrap='true'><a href='" + rs.Fields(x).Value + "'>"
+ rs.Fields(x).Value + "</a></td>")
```

Listbox

```
        txtstream.WriteLine("<td  style=""font-family:Calibri, Sans-Serif;font-size:
12px;color:navy;""  align='left'  nowrap='true'><select multiple><option value = """
+ rs.Fields(x).Value + """>" + rs.Fields(x).Value + "</option></select></td>")
```

Span

```
        txtstream.WriteLine("<td  style="""font-family:Calibri,  Sans-Serif;font-
size: 12px;color:navy;"" align='left' nowrap='true'><span>" + rs.Fields(x).Value
+ "</span></td>")
```

Textarea

```
        txtstream.WriteLine("<td  style="""font-family:Calibri,  Sans-Serif;font-size:
12px;color:navy;""  align='left'  nowrap='true'><textarea>"  +  rs.Fields(x).Value  +
"</textarea></td>")
```

Textbox

```
        txtstream.WriteLine("<td  style="""font-family:Calibri,  Sans-Serif;font-
size: 12px;color:navy;""  align='left'  nowrap='true'><input  type=text  value="""  +
rs.Fields(x).Value + """"></input></td>")
        rs.MoveNext

    txtstream.WriteLine("</tr>")

txtstream.WriteLine("</table>")
txtstream.WriteLine("</body>")
txtstream.WriteLine("</html>")
txtstream.Close()
```

Horizontal Tables

```
    txtstream.WriteLine("<table      style='border:Double;border-width:1px;border-
color:navy;' rules=all frames=both cellpadding=2 cellspacing=2 Width=0>")
    txtstream.WriteLine("<tr>")
    for x = 0 in rs.fields.count:
```

64

txtstream.WriteLine("<th style="" font-family:Calibri, Sans-Serif;font-size: 12px;color:darkred;"" align='left' nowrap='nowrap'>" + rs.Fields(x).Name + "</th>")

while rs.eof = false:
   txtstream.WriteLine("<tr>")
     for x = 0 in rs.fields.count:

NONE

txtstream.WriteLine("<td style=""font-family:Calibri, Sans-Serif;font-size: 12px;color:navy;"" align='left' nowrap='nowrap'>" + rs.Fields(x).Value + "</td>")

Button

txtstream.WriteLine("<td style=""font-family:Calibri, Sans-Serif;font-size: 12px;color:navy;"" align='left' nowrap='true'><button style='width:100%;' value ='" + rs.Fields(x).Value + "'>" + rs.Fields(x).Value + "</button></td>")

COMBOBOX

txtstream.WriteLine("<td style=""font-family:Calibri, Sans-Serif;font-size: 12px;color:navy;"" align='left' nowrap='true'><select><option value = """ + rs.Fields(x).Value + """">" + rs.Fields(x).Value + "</option></select></td>")

DIV

txtstream.WriteLine("<td style=""font-family:Calibri, Sans-Serif;font-size: 12px;color:navy;"" align='left' nowrap='true'> " + rs.Fields(x).Value + " </td>")

LINK

txtstream.WriteLine("<td style=""font-family:Calibri, Sans-Serif;font-size: 12px;color:navy;"" align='left' nowrap='true'><a href='" + rs.Fields(x).Value + "'>" + rs.Fields(x).Value + "</a></td>")

LISTBOX

txtstream.WriteLine("<td style=""font-family:Calibri, Sans-Serif;font-size: 12px;color:navy;"" align='left' nowrap='true'><select multiple><option value = """" + rs.Fields(x).Value + """">" + rs.Fields(x).Value + "</option></select></td>")

SPAN

txtstream.WriteLine("<td style=""font-family:Calibri, Sans-Serif;font-size: 12px;color:navy;"" align='left' nowrap='true'>" + rs.Fields(x).Value + "</td>")

TEXTAREA

txtstream.WriteLine("<td style=""font-family:Calibri, Sans-Serif;font-size: 12px;color:navy;"" align='left' nowrap='true'><textarea>" + rs.Fields(x).Value + "</textarea></td>")

TEXTBOX

```
            txtstream.WriteLine("<td style=""font-family:Calibri, Sans-Serif;font-
size: 12px;color:navy;"" align='left' nowrap='true'><input type=text value=""" +
rs.Fields(x).Value + """></input></td>")

        txtstream.WriteLine("</tr>")
        rs.MoveNext

    txtstream.WriteLine("</table>")
    txtstream.WriteLine("</body>")
    txtstream.WriteLine("</html>")
    txtstream.Close()
```

Vertical Tables

```
    txtstream.WriteLine("<table     style='border:Double;border-width:1px;border-
color:navy;' rules=all frames=both cellpadding=2 cellspacing=2 Width=0>")
    for x = 0 in rs.fields.count:
        txtstream.WriteLine("<tr><th      style=""  font-family:Calibri,   Sans-
Serif;font-size:  12px;color:darkred;""    align='left'   nowrap='nowrap'>"   +
rs.Fields(x).Name + "</th>")
        rs.MoveFirst()
        while rs.eof == False:
            txtstream.WriteLine("<td  style=""font-family:Calibri,  Sans-Serif;font-
size: 12px;color:navy;"">" + rs.Fields(x).Value + "</td>")
```

NONE

```
        txtstream.WriteLine("<td  style=""font-family:Calibri,  Sans-Serif;font-
size: 12px;color:navy;""  align='left'  nowrap='nowrap'>"  +  rs.Fields(x).Value  +
"</td>")
```

Button

txtstream.WriteLine("<td style=""font-family:Calibri, Sans-Serif;font-size: 12px;color:navy;"" align='left' nowrap='true'><button style='width:100%;' value ='" + rs.Fields(x).Value + "'>" + rs.Fields(x).Value + "</button></td>")

Combobox

txtstream.WriteLine("<td style=""font-family:Calibri, Sans-Serif;font-size: 12px;color:navy;"" align='left' nowrap='true'><select><option value = """ + rs.Fields(x).Value + """>" + rs.Fields(x).Value + "</option></select></td>")

Div

txtstream.WriteLine("<td style=""font-family:Calibri, Sans-Serif;font-size: 12px;color:navy;"" align='left' nowrap='true'> " + rs.Fields(x).Value + " </td>")

Link

txtstream.WriteLine("<td style=""font-family:Calibri, Sans-Serif;font-size: 12px;color:navy;"" align='left' nowrap='true'><a href='" + rs.Fields(x).Value + "'>" + rs.Fields(x).Value + "</a></td>")

Listbox

txtstream.WriteLine("<td style=""font-family:Calibri, Sans-Serif;font-size: 12px;color:navy;"" align='left' nowrap='true'><select multiple><option value = """ + rs.Fields(x).Value + """>" + rs.Fields(x).Value + "</option></select></td>")

Span

```
txtstream.WriteLine("<td    style=""font-family:Calibri,  Sans-Serif;font-
size: 12px;color:navy;""" align='left' nowrap='true'><span>" + rs.Fields(x).Value
+ "</span></td>")
```

Textarea

```
txtstream.WriteLine("<td  style=""font-family:Calibri,  Sans-Serif;font-size:
12px;color:navy;""" align='left' nowrap='true'><textarea>" + rs.Fields(x).Value +
"</textarea></td>")
```

Textbox

```
txtstream.WriteLine("<td    style=""font-family:Calibri,  Sans-Serif;font-
size: 12px;color:navy;""" align='left' nowrap='true'><input type=text value=""" +
rs.Fields(x).Value + """></input></td>")
        rs.MoveNext

    txtstream.WriteLine("</tr>")

    txtstream.WriteLine("</table>")
    txtstream.WriteLine("</body>")
    txtstream.WriteLine("</html>")
    txtstream.Close()
```

Delimited Files

Chapter Subtitle

Chapter Epigraph uses a quote or verse to

introduce the chapter and set the stage.

—Attribute the quote

T—HERE ARE MANY DIFFERENT KINDS OF DELIMITED FILES. The ones we are going to be using are the most common ones. And by Common, this will include:

- Colon Delimited
- Comma Delimited
- Exclamation Delimited
- Semi-Colon Delimited
- Tab Delimited
- Tilde Delimited

Essentially, the only differences in the code is how the delimiter is used, but the code examples are also going to show you how the information can be arranged in both Horizontal and Vertical Views.

Colon Delimited Horizontal View

```
ws = win32com.client.Dispatch("WScript.Shell")
fso = win32com.client.Dispatch("Scripting.FileSystemObject")
txtstream = fso.OpenTextFile(ws.CurrentDirectory + "\Products.txt", 2, True,
-2)
    tstr= ""
Horizontal
    for x = 0 in rs.fields.count:
        if tstr <> "":
            tstr = tstr + ":"

        tstr = tstr + rs.Fields(x).Name

    txtstream.Writeline(tstr)
    tstr = ""
    rs.MoveFirst()
    while rs.eof = false:
        for x = 0 in rs.fields.count:
            if tstr <> "":
                tstr = tstr + ":"

            tstr = tstr + '"' + rs.Fields(x).Value + '"'

        txtstream.Writeline(tstr)
        tstr = ""
        rs.MoveNext
```

Colon Delimited Vertical View

```
    for x = 0 in rs.fields.count:
```

```
        tstr = rs.Fields(x).Name
        rs.MoveFirst()
        while rs.eof = false:
            if tstr <> "":
                tstr = tstr + ":"

            tstr = tstr + '"' + rs.Fields(x).Value + '"'
            rs.MoveNext

        txtstream.Writeline(tstr)
        tstr = ""

        txtstream.Close
```

Comma Delimited Horizontal

```
    ws = win32com.client.Dispatch("WScript.Shell")
    fso = win32com.client.Dispatch("Scripting.FileSystemObject")
    txtstream = fso.OpenTextFile(ws.CurrentDirectory + "\Products.csv", 2,
True, -2)
        tstr= ""
Horizontal
    for x = 0 in rs.fields.count:
        if tstr <> "":
            tstr = tstr + ","

        tstr = tstr + rs.Fields(x).Name

    txtstream.Writeline(tstr)
    tstr = ""
    rs.MoveFirst()
    while rs.eof = false:
```

```
for x = 0 in rs.fields.count:
    if tstr <> "":
        tstr = tstr + ","

    tstr = tstr + '"' + rs.Fields(x).Value + '"'

    txtstream.Writeline(tstr)
    tstr = ""
    rs.MoveNext
```

Comma Delimited Vertical

```
for x = 0 in rs.fields.count:
    tstr = rs.Fields(x).Name
    rs.MoveFirst()
    while rs.eof = false:
        if tstr <> "":
            tstr = tstr + ","

        tstr = tstr + '"' + rs.Fields(x).Value + '"'
        rs.MoveNext

    txtstream.Writeline(tstr)
    tstr = ""


txtstream.Close
```

Exclamation Delimited Horizontal

```
ws = win32com.client.Dispatch("WScript.Shell")
fso = win32com.client.Dispatch("Scripting.FileSystemObject")
txtstream = fso.OpenTextFile(ws.CurrentDirectory + "\Products.txt", 2, True,
-2)
    tstr= ""
Horizontal
    for x = 0 in rs.fields.count:
        if tstr <> "":
            tstr = tstr + "!"

        tstr = tstr + rs.Fields(x).Name

    txtstream.Writeline(tstr)
    tstr = ""
    rs.MoveFirst()
    while rs.eof = false:
        for x = 0 in rs.fields.count:
            if tstr <> "":
                tstr = tstr + "!"

            tstr = tstr + '"' + rs.Fields(x).Value + '"'

        txtstream.Writeline(tstr)
        tstr = ""
        rs.MoveNext
```

Exclamation Delimited Vertical

```
    for x = 0 in rs.fields.count:
```

```
        tstr = rs.Fields(x).Name
        rs.MoveFirst()
        while rs.eof = false:
            if tstr <> "":
                tstr = tstr + "!"

            tstr = tstr + '"' + rs.Fields(x).Value + '"'
            rs.MoveNext

        txtstream.Writeline(tstr)
        tstr = ""


        txtstream.Close
```

Semi Colon Delimited Horizontal

```
    ws = win32com.client.Dispatch("WScript.Shell")
    fso = win32com.client.Dispatch("Scripting.FileSystemObject")
    txtstream = fso.OpenTextFile(ws.CurrentDirectory + "\Products.txt", 2, True,
-2)
        tstr= ""
    Horizontal
        for x = 0 in rs.fields.count:
            if tstr <> "":
                tstr = tstr + ";"

            tstr = tstr + rs.Fields(x).Name

        txtstream.Writeline(tstr)
        tstr = ""
        rs.MoveFirst()
        while rs.eof = false:
```

```
for x = 0 in rs.fields.count:
    if tstr <> "":
        tstr = tstr + ";"

    tstr = tstr + '"' + rs.Fields(x).Value + '"'

    txtstream.Writeline(tstr)
    tstr = ""
    rs.MoveNext
```

Semi Colon Delimited Vertical

```
for x = 0 in rs.fields.count:
    tstr = rs.Fields(x).Name
    rs.MoveFirst()
    while rs.eof = false:
        if tstr <> "":
            tstr = tstr + ";"

        tstr = tstr + '"' + rs.Fields(x).Value + '"'
        rs.MoveNext

    txtstream.Writeline(tstr)
    tstr = ""


    txtstream.Close
```

Tab Delimited Horizontal

```
        ws = win32com.client.Dispatch("WScript.Shell")
        fso = win32com.client.Dispatch("Scripting.FileSystemObject")
        txtstream = fso.OpenTextFile(ws.CurrentDirectory + "\Products.txt", 2, True,
-2)
        tstr= ""

        for x = 0 in rs.fields.count:
           if tstr <> "":
              tstr = tstr + vbtab

           tstr = tstr + rs.Fields(x).Name

        txtstream.Writeline(tstr)
        tstr = ""
        rs.MoveFirst()
        while rs.eof = false:
           for x = 0 in rs.fields.count:
              if tstr <> "":
                 tstr = tstr + vbtab

              tstr = tstr + '"' + rs.Fields(x).Value + '"'

           txtstream.Writeline(tstr)
           tstr = ""
           rs.MoveNext
```

Tab Delimited Vertical

```
        for x = 0 in rs.fields.count:
           tstr = rs.Fields(x).Name
           rs.MoveFirst()
           while rs.eof = false:
              if tstr <> "":
```

```
            tstr = tstr + vbtab

        tstr = tstr + '"' + rs.Fields(x).Value + '"'
        rs.MoveNext

    txtstream.Writeline(tstr)
    tstr = ""



    txtstream.Close
```

Tilde Delimited Horizontal

```
    ws = win32com.client.Dispatch("WScript.Shell")
    fso = win32com.client.Dispatch("Scripting.FileSystemObject")
    txtstream = fso.OpenTextFile(ws.CurrentDirectory + "\Products.txt", 2, True,
-2)
    tstr= ""
Horizontal
    for x = 0 in rs.fields.count:
      if tstr <> "":
        tstr = tstr + "~"

      tstr = tstr + rs.Fields(x).Name

    txtstream.Writeline(tstr)
    tstr = ""
    rs.MoveFirst()
    while rs.eof = false:
      for x = 0 in rs.fields.count:
        if tstr <> "":
```

```
            tstr = tstr + "~"

         tstr = tstr + '"' + rs.Fields(x).Value + '"'

      txtstream.Writeline(tstr)
      tstr = ""
      rs.MoveNext
```

Tilde Delimited Vertical

```
   for x = 0 in rs.fields.count:
      tstr = rs.Fields(x).Name
      rs.MoveFirst()
      while rs.eof = false:
         if tstr <> "":
            tstr = tstr + "~"

         tstr = tstr + '"' + rs.Fields(x).Value + '"'
         rs.MoveNext

      txtstream.Writeline(tstr)
      tstr = ""

      txtstream.Close
```

XML Files

In this section of the book, we're going to be Coding for the creation of Attribute XML Element XML, Element XML for XSL and Schema XML

```
import win32com.client
import string
```

Attribute XML Using A Text file

```
ws  = Win32com.client.Dispatch("WScript.Shell")
fso = Win32com.client.Dispatch("Scripting.FileSystemObject")
txtstream = fso.OpenTextFile("C:\Products.xml", 2, True, -2)
txtstream.WriteLine("<?xml version='1.0' encoding='iso-8859-1'?>")
txtstream.WriteLine("<data>")
rs.MoveFirst()
While rs.EOF = false:
    txtstream.WriteLine("<Products>")
    For x in range(rs.Fields.Count):
        txtstream.WriteLine("<property name = """ + rs.Fields[x].Name + """
value=""" + rs.Fields[x].value + """/>")
```

```
    txtstream.WriteLine("</Products>")
rs.MoveNext()

txtstream.WriteLine("</data>")
txtstream.Close
```

Attribute XML Using the DOM

```
    xmldoc = win32com.client.Dispatch("MSXML2.DOMDocument")
    pi      =      xmldoc.CreateProcessingInstruction("xml",      "version='1.0'
encoding='ISO-8859-1'")
    oRoot = xmldoc.CreateElement("data")
    xmldoc.AppendChild(pi)
    while rs.EOF  == False:
      oNode = xmldoc.CreateNode(1, "Win32_Process", "")
      for x in range(rs.Fields.Count):
        oNode1 = xmldoc.CreateNode(1, "Property", "")
        oAtt = xmldoc.CreateAttribute("NAME")
        oAtt.Value = rs.Fields[x].Name
        oNode1.Attributes.SetNamedItem(oAtt)
        oAtt = xmldoc.CreateAttribute("DATATYPE")
        oAtt.Value = str(rs.Fields[x].Type.Name))
        oNode1.Attributes.SetNamedItem(oAtt)
        oAtt = xmldoc.CreateAttribute("SIZE")
        oAtt.Value = str(rs.Fields[x].Value.)
        oNode1.Attributes.SetNamedItem(oAtt)
        oAtt = xmldoc.CreateAttribute("Value")
        oAtt.Value = GetValue(prop, obj)
        oNode1.Attributes.SetNamedItem(oAtt)
        oNode.AppendChild(oNode1)
```

```
        oRoot.AppendChild(oNode)

    xmldoc.AppendChild(oRoot)
    ws = win32com.client.Dispatch("WScript.Shell")
    xmldoc.Save(ws.CurrentDirectory + "\\Products.xml")
```

Element XML Using A Text file

```
    ws = win32com.client.Dispatch("WScript.Shell")
    fso = win32com.client.Dispatch("Scripting.FileSystemObject")
    txtstream = fso.OpenTextFile(ws.CurrentDirectory + "\Products.txt", 2, True,
-2)
    txtstream.WriteLine("<?xml version='1.0' encoding='iso-8859-1'?>")
    txtstream.WriteLine("<data>")
    rs.MoveFirst
    while rs.eof = false:
        txtstream.WriteLine("<Products>")
        for x = 0 in rs.fields.count:
            txtstream.WriteLine("<" + rs.Fields(x).Name + ">" + rs.Fields(x).Value
+ "</" + rs.Fields(x).Name + ">")

        txtstream.WriteLine("</Products>")
        rs.MoveNext()

    txtstream.WriteLine("</data>")
    txtstream.close()
```

Element XML Using the DOM

```
xmldoc  = win32com.client.Dispatch("MSXML2.DOMDocument")
pi      =      xmldoc.CreateProcessingInstruction("xml",      "version='1.0'
encoding='ISO-8859-1'")
oRoot = xmldoc.CreateElement("data")
xmldoc.AppendChild(pi)
while rs.EOF == False:
  oNode = xmldoc.CreateNode(1, "Win32_Process", "")
  for x in range(rs.Fields.Count):
    oNode1 = xmldoc.CreateNode(1, rs.Fields[x],Name, "")
    oNode1.Text = str(rs.Fields[x].Value)
    oNode.AppendChild(oNode1)

  oRoot.AppendChild(oNode)

xmldoc.AppendChild(oRoot)
ws = win32com.client.Dispatch("WScript.Shell")
xmldoc.Save(ws.CurrentDirectory + "\\Products.xml")
```

Element XML FOR XSL Using A Text File

```
ws = win32com.client.Dispatch("WScript.Shell")
fso = win32com.client.Dispatch("Scripting.FileSystemObject")
txtstream = fso.OpenTextFile(ws.CurrentDirectory + "\Products.txt", 2, True,
-2)
txtstream.WriteLine("<?xml version='1.0' encoding='iso-8859-1'?>")
```

```
    txtstream.WriteLine("<?xml-stylesheet     type='Text/xsl'     href='"     +
ws.CurrentDirectory + "\Products.xsl"?>
    rs.MoveFirst
    while rs.eof = false:
        txtstream.WriteLine("<Products>")
        for x = 0 in rs.fields.count:
            txtstream.WriteLine("<" + rs.Fields(x).Name + ">" + rs.Fields(x).Value
+ "</" + rs.Fields(x).Name + ">")

        txtstream.WriteLine("</Products>")
        rs.MoveNext()

    txtstream.WriteLine("</data>")
    txtstream.close()
```

Element XML FOR XSL Using The DOM

```
xmldoc = win32com.client.Dispatch("MSXML2.DOMDocument")
pi = xmldoc.CreateProcessingInstruction("xml", "version='1.0' encoding='ISO-
8859-1'")
pii = xmldoc.CreateProcessingInstruction("xml-stylesheet", "type='text/xsl'
href='Process.xsl'")
oRoot = xmldoc.CreateElement("data")
xmldoc.AppendChild(pi)
xmldoc.AppendChild(pii)

    while rs.EOF == False:
        oNode = xmldoc.CreateNode(1, "Win32_Process", "")
        for x in range(rs.Fields.Count):
            oNode1 = xmldoc.CreateNode(1, rs.Fields[x],Name, "")
            oNode1.Text = str(rs.Fields[x].Value)
            oNode.AppendChild(oNode1)
```

```
        oRoot.AppendChild(oNode)


    xmldoc.AppendChild(oRoot)
    ws = win32com.client.Dispatch("WScript.Shell")
    xmldoc.Save(ws.CurrentDirectory + "\\Products.xml")
```

Schema XML Using A Text File

```
    ws = win32com.client.Dispatch("WScript.Shell")
    fso = win32com.client.Dispatch("Scripting.FileSystemObject")
    txtstream = fso.OpenTextFile(ws.CurrentDirectory + "\Products.txt", 2, True,
-2)
    txtstream.WriteLine("<?xml version='1.0' encoding='iso-8859-1'?>")
    txtstream.WriteLine("<data>")
    rs.MoveFirst
    while rs.eof = false:
        txtstream.WriteLine("<Products>")
        for x = 0 in rs.fields.count:
            txtstream.WriteLine("<" + rs.Fields(x).Name + ">" + rs.Fields(x).Value
+ "</" + rs.Fields(x).Name + ">")

        txtstream.WriteLine("</Products>")
        rs.MoveNext()

    txtstream.WriteLine("</data>")
    txtstream.close()

    rs1 = win32com.client.Dispatch("ADODB.Recordset")
    rs1.ActiveConnection        =        "Provider=MSDAOSP;        Data
Source=msxml2.DSOControl"
    rs1.Open(ws.CurrentDirectory + "\Products.xml")
```

```
        If (fso.FileExists(ws.CurrentDirectory + "\Products_Schema.xml") = True)
Then
            fso.DeleteFile(ws.CurrentDirectory + "\Products_Schema.xml")


        rs.Save(ws.CurrentDirectory + "\Products_Schema.xml", 1)
```

Schema XML Using the DOM

```
        xmldoc = win32com.client.Dispatch("MSXML2.DOMDocument")
        pi    =    xmldoc.CreateProcessingInstruction("xml",    "version='1.0'
encoding='ISO-8859-1'")
        oRoot = xmldoc.CreateElement("data")
        xmldoc.AppendChild(pi)
        while rs.EOF == False:
          oNode = xmldoc.CreateNode(1, "Win32_Process", "")
          for x in range(rs.Fields.Count):
            oNode1 = xmldoc.CreateNode(1, rs.Fields[x],Name, "")
            oNode1.Text = str(rs.Fields[x].Value)
            oNode.AppendChild(oNode1)

          oRoot.AppendChild(oNode)

        xmldoc.AppendChild(oRoot)
        ws = win32com.client.Dispatch("WScript.Shell")
        xmldoc.Save(ws.CurrentDirectory + "\\Products.xml")


        rs1 = win32com.client.Dispatch("ADODB.Recordset")
        rs1.ActiveConnection          =          "Provider=MSDAOSP;          Data
Source=msxml2.DSOControl"
        rs1.Open(ws.CurrentDirectory + "\Products.xml")
```

```
        If (fso.FileExists(ws.CurrentDirectory + "\Products_Schema.xml") = True)
Then
            fso.DeleteFile(ws.CurrentDirectory + "\Products_Schema.xml")


        rs.Save(ws.CurrentDirectory + "\Products_Schema.xml", 1)
```

Excel Coding Examples

B ELOW ARE SOME EXAMPLES OF ADO DRIVING EXCEL VISUAL RENDERINGS.

Excel Code in Horizontal Format using a CSV File

```
ws = win32com.client.Dispatch("WScript.Shell")
fso = win32com.client.Dispatch("Scripting.FileSystemObject")
txtstream = fso.OpenTextFile(ws.CurrentDirectory + "\Products.csv", 2,
True, -2)
    tstr= ""


for x = 0 in rs.fields.count:
  if tstr <> "":
    tstr = tstr + ","

  tstr = tstr + rs.Fields(x).Name

txtstream.Writeline(tstr)
tstr = ""
rs.MoveFirst()
while rs.eof = false:
```

```
    for x = 0 in rs.fields.count:
        if tstr <> "":
            tstr = tstr + ","

        tstr = tstr + '"' + rs.Fields(x).Value + '"'

    txtstream.Writeline(tstr)
    tstr = ""
    rs.MoveNext
```

Excel Code in Vertical Format using a CSV File

```
    ws = win32com.client.Dispatch("WScript.Shell")
    fso = win32com.client.Dispatch("Scripting.FileSystemObject")
    txtstream = fso.OpenTextFile(ws.CurrentDirectory + "\Products.csv", 2,
True, -2)
    tstr= ""


    for x = 0 in rs.fields.count:
        tstr = rs.Fields(x).Name
        rs.MoveFirst()
        while rs.eof = false:
            if tstr <> "":
                tstr = tstr + ","

            tstr = tstr + '"' + rs.Fields(x).Value + '"'
            rs.MoveNext

        txtstream.Writeline(tstr)
        tstr = ""

    txtstream.Close
```

```
ws.Run(ws.CurrentDirectory + "\Products.csv")
```

Excel using Horizontal Format Automation Code

```
oExcel = win32com.client.Dispatch("Excel.Application")
oExcel.Visible = true
wb = oExcel.Workbooks.Add()
ws = wb.WorkSheets(1)
ws.Name = "Products"
x=1
y=2
for z in 1..rs.fields.count-1 do
    ws.Cells.Item(1, x) = rs.Fields(z).Name
    x=x+1

x=1
rs.MoveFirst()
Do While rs.EOF = False
    for z in 1..rs.fields.count-1 do
        ws.Cells.Item(y, x) = rs.Fields(z).Value
        x=x+1

    x=1
    y=y+1
    rs.MoveNext


ws.Columns.HorizontalAlignment = -4131
iret = ws.Columns.AutoFit()
```

Excel using Vertical Format Automation Code

```
oExcel = win32com.client.Dispatch("Excel.Application")
oExcel.Visible = true
wb = oExcel.Workbooks.Add()
ws = wb.WorkSheets(1)
ws.Name = "Products"
x=1
y=2
for z in 1..rs.fields.count-1 do
   ws.Cells.Item(x, 1) = rs.Fields(z).Name
   x=x+1

x=1
rs.MoveFirst()
Do While rs.EOF = False
   for z in 1..rs.fields.count-1 do
      ws.Cells.Item(x, y) = rs.Fields(z).Value
      x=x+1

   x=1
   y=y+1
   rs.MoveNext


ws.Columns.HorizontalAlignment = -4131
iret = ws.Columns.AutoFit()
```

Excel Spreadsheet Example

```
ws = win32com.client.Dispatch("WScript.Shell")
fso = win32com.client.Dispatch("Scripting.FileSystemObject")
txtstream = fso.OpenTextFile(ws.CurrentDirectory + "\\ProcessExcel.xml", 2,
True, -2)
txtstream.WriteLine("<?xml version='1.0'?>")
txtstream.WriteLine("<?mso-application progid='Excel.Sheet'?>")
txtstream.WriteLine("<Workbook             xmlns='urn:schemas-microsoft-
com:office:spreadsheet'        xmlns:o='urn:schemas-microsoft-com:office:office'
xmlns:x='urn:schemas-microsoft-com:office:excel'          xmlns:ss='urn:schemas-
microsoft-com:office:spreadsheet'        xmlns:html='http://www.w3.org/TR/REC-
html40'>")
txtstream.WriteLine("        <DocumentProperties         xmlns='urn:schemas-
microsoft-com:office:office'>")
txtstream.WriteLine("                <Author>Windows User</Author>")
txtstream.WriteLine("                <LastAuthor>Windows
User</LastAuthor>")
txtstream.WriteLine("                <Created>2007-11-
27T19:36:16Z</Created>")
txtstream.WriteLine("                <Version>12.00</Version>")
txtstream.WriteLine("        </DocumentProperties>")
txtstream.WriteLine("        <ExcelWorkbook            xmlns='urn:schemas-
microsoft-com:office:excel'>")
txtstream.WriteLine("
  <WindowHeight>11835</WindowHeight>")
txtstream.WriteLine("
  <WindowWidth>18960</WindowWidth>")
txtstream.WriteLine("              <WindowTopX>120</WindowTopX>")
txtstream.WriteLine("              <WindowTopY>135</WindowTopY>")
txtstream.WriteLine("
  <ProtectStructure>False</ProtectStructure>")
txtstream.WriteLine("
  <ProtectWindows>False</ProtectWindows>")
txtstream.WriteLine("          </ExcelWorkbook>")
```

```
txtstream.WriteLine("          <Styles>")
txtstream.WriteLine("              <Style                ss:ID='Default'
ss:Name='Normal'>")
txtstream.WriteLine("                  <Alignment
ss:Vertical='Bottom'/>")
txtstream.WriteLine("                  <Borders/>")
txtstream.WriteLine("                  <Font    ss:FontName='Calibri'
x:Family='Swiss' ss:Size='11' ss:Color='#000000'/>")
txtstream.WriteLine("                  <Interior/>")
txtstream.WriteLine("                  <NumberFormat/>")
txtstream.WriteLine("                  <Protection/>")
txtstream.WriteLine("              </Style>")
txtstream.WriteLine("              <Style ss:ID='s62'>")
txtstream.WriteLine("                  <Borders/>")
txtstream.WriteLine("                  <Font    ss:FontName='Calibri'
x:Family='Swiss' ss:Size='11' ss:Color='#000000' ss:Bold='1'/>")
txtstream.WriteLine("              </Style>")
txtstream.WriteLine("              <Style ss:ID='s63'>")
txtstream.WriteLine("                  <Alignment
ss:Horizontal='Left' ss:Vertical='Bottom' ss:Indent='2'/>")
txtstream.WriteLine("                  <Font  ss:FontName='Verdana'
x:Family='Swiss' ss:Size='7.7' ss:Color='#000000'/>")
txtstream.WriteLine("              </Style>")
txtstream.WriteLine("  </Styles>")

txtstream.WriteLine("<Worksheet ss:Name='Process'>")
txtstream.WriteLine("          <Table    x:FullColumns='1'    x:FullRows='1'
ss:DefaultRowHeight='24.9375'>")
txtstream.WriteLine("          <Column  ss:AutoFitWidth='1' ss:Width='82.5'
ss:Span='5'/>")
txtstream.WriteLine("     <Row ss:AutoFitHeight='0'>")
for x in range(rs.Fields.Count):
```

93

```python
        txtstream.WriteLine("                        <Cell   ss:StyleID='s62'><Data
ss:Type='String'>" + rs.Fields[x].Name + "</Data></Cell>")

        txtstream.WriteLine("      </Row>")

    while rs.EOF == False:
        txtstream.WriteLine("      <Row ss:AutoFitHeight='0' ss:Height='13.5'>")
        for x in range(rs.Fields.Count):
            txtstream.WriteLine("           <Cell><Data ss:Type='String'><![CDATA[" +
str(rs.Fields[x].Value)) + "]]></Data></Cell>")

        txtstream.WriteLine("      </Row>")


    txtstream.WriteLine("  </Table>")
    txtstream.WriteLine("          <WorksheetOptions          xmlns='urn:schemas-
microsoft-com:office:excel'>")
    txtstream.WriteLine("                    <PageSetup>")
    txtstream.WriteLine("                        <Header x:Margin='0.3'/>")
    txtstream.WriteLine("                        <Footer x:Margin='0.3'/>")
    txtstream.WriteLine("                        <PageMargins x:Bottom='0.75'
x:Left='0.7' x:Right='0.7' x:Top='0.75'/>")
    txtstream.WriteLine("                    </PageSetup>")
    txtstream.WriteLine("                    <Unsynced/>")
    txtstream.WriteLine("                    <Print>")
    txtstream.WriteLine("                        <FitHeight>0</FitHeight>")
    txtstream.WriteLine("                        <ValidPrinterInfo/>")
    txtstream.WriteLine("
    <HorizontalResolution>600</HorizontalResolution>")
    txtstream.WriteLine("
    <VerticalResolution>600</VerticalResolution>")
    txtstream.WriteLine("                    </Print>")
    txtstream.WriteLine("                    <Selected/>")
```

```
txtstream.WriteLine("                        <Panes>")
txtstream.WriteLine("                            <Pane>")
txtstream.WriteLine("
   <Number>3</Number>")
txtstream.WriteLine("
   <ActiveRow>9</ActiveRow>")
txtstream.WriteLine("
   <ActiveCol>7</ActiveCol>")
txtstream.WriteLine("                            </Pane>")
txtstream.WriteLine("                    </Panes>")
txtstream.WriteLine("
   <ProtectObjects>False</ProtectObjects>")
txtstream.WriteLine("
   <ProtectScenarios>False</ProtectScenarios>")
txtstream.WriteLine("           </WorksheetOptions>")
txtstream.WriteLine("</Worksheet>")
txtstream.WriteLine("</Workbook>")
txtstream.Close()
ws.Run(ws.CurrentDirectory + "\\Products.xml")
```

Creating XSL Files

BELOW are examples of creating XSL files.

```
ws = win32com.client.Dispatch("WScript.Shell")
fso = win32com.client.Dispatch("Scripting.FileSystemObject")
txtstream = fso.OpenTextFile(ws.CurrentDirectory + "\Products.xsl", 2, true, -2)
txtstream.WriteLine("<?xml version='1.0' encoding='UTF-8'?>")
txtstream.WriteLine("<xsl:stylesheet                    version='1.0'
xmlns:xsl='http://www.w3.org/1999/XSL/Transform'>")
txtstream.WriteLine("<xsl:template match=""/"">")
txtstream.WriteLine("<html>")
txtstream.WriteLine("<head>")
txtstream.WriteLine("<title>Products</title>")
txtstream.WriteLine("</head>")
#Add Stylesheet Here
txtstream.WriteLine("<body>")
rs.MoveFirst()
```

Single Line Horizontal Reports

txtstream.WriteLine("<table border='0' Cellpadding='2' cellspacing='2>")

txtstream.WriteLine("<tr>")
for x = 0 to rs.Fields.count-1
    txtstream.WriteLine("<th align='left' nowrap='true'>" + rs.Fields(x).Name
+ "</th>")

txtstream.WriteLine("</tr>")
txtstream.WriteLine("<tr>")
for x = 0 to rs.Fields.count-1

NONE
txtstream.WriteLine("<td><xsl:value-of   select=""data/Products/"   +
rs.Fields(x).Name + """/></td>")

BUTTON

txtstream.WriteLine("<td   align='left'   nowrap='true'><button
style='width:100%;'><xsl:value-of select=""data/Products/" + rs.Fields(x).Name +
"""/></button></td>")

COMBOBOX

txtstream.WriteLine("<td   align='left'
nowrap='true'><select><option><xsl:attribute   name='value'><xsl:value-of
select=""data/Products/" + rs.Fields(x).Name + """/></xsl:attribute><xsl:value-of
select=""data/Products/" + rs.Fields(x).Name + """/></option></select></td>")

DIV

```
txtstream.WriteLine("<td   align='left' nowrap='true'><div><xsl:value-
of select=""data/Products/" + rs.Fields(x).Name + """/></div></td>")
```

LINK

```
txtstream.WriteLine("<td   align='left' nowrap='true'><a href='" +
rs.Fields(x).Value + "'><xsl:value-of select=""data/Products/" + rs.Fields(x).Name
+ """/></a></td>")
```

LISTBOX

```
txtstream.WriteLine("<td          align='left'      nowrap='true'><select
multiple><option><xsl:attribute                    name='value'><xsl:value-of
select=""data/Products/" + rs.Fields(x).Name  + """/></xsl:attribute><xsl:value-of
select=""data/Products/" + rs.Fields(x).Name + """/></option></select></td>")
```

SPAN

```
txtstream.WriteLine("<td                                align='left'
nowrap='true'><span><xsl:value-of select=""data/Products/" + rs.Fields(x).Name  +
"""/></span></td>")
```

TEXTAREA

```
txtstream.WriteLine("<td                                align='left'
nowrap='true'><textarea><xsl:value-of         select=""data/Products/"       +
rs.Fields(x).Name  + """/></textarea></td>")
```

TEXTBOX

txtstream.WriteLine("<td   align='left'   nowrap='true'><input type='text'><xsl:attribute name=""value""><xsl:value-of select=""data/Products/" + rs.Fields(x).Name + """/></xsl:attribute></input></td>")

txtstream.WriteLine("</tr>")

Multi Line Horizontal Reports

txtstream.WriteLine("<table border='0' Cellpadding='2' cellspacing='2>")

txtstream.WriteLine("<tr>")
for x = 0 to rs.Fields.count-1
    txtstream.WriteLine("<th>" + rs.Fields(x).Name + "</th>")

txtstream.WriteLine("</tr>")
txtstream.WriteLine("<xsl:for-each select=""data/Products"">")
txtstream.WriteLine("<tr>")
for x = 0 to rs.Fields.count-1
    txtstream.WriteLine("<td><xsl:value-of select="" " + rs.Fields(x).Name + " ""/></td>")

NONE

txtstream.WriteLine("<td><xsl:value-of select=""" + rs.Fields(x).Name + """/></td>")

BUTTON

txtstream.WriteLine("<td   align='left'   nowrap='true'><button style='width:100%;'><xsl:value-of   select='"""   +   rs.Fields(x).Name   + """'/></button></td>")

COMBOBOX

txtstream.WriteLine("<td   align='left' nowrap='true'><select><option><xsl:attribute   name='value'><xsl:value-of select='"""   +   rs.Fields(x).Name   +   """'/></xsl:attribute><xsl:value-of select='""data/Products/" + rs.Fields(x).Name + """'/></option></select></td>")

DIV

txtstream.WriteLine("<td   align='left' nowrap='true'> <xsl:value-of select='""data/Products/" + rs.Fields(x).Name + """'/> </td>")

LINK

txtstream.WriteLine("<td   align='left' nowrap='true'><a href='" + rs.Fields(x).Value + "'><xsl:value-of select='""data/Products/" + rs.Fields(x).Name + """'/></a></td>")

LISTBOX

txtstream.WriteLine("<td   align='left'   nowrap='true'><select multiple><option><xsl:attribute   name='value'><xsl:value-of select='""data/Products/" + rs.Fields(x).Name + """'/></xsl:attribute><xsl:value-of select='""data/Products/" + rs.Fields(x).Name + """'/></option></select></td>")

SPAN

```
        txtstream.WriteLine("<td                              align='left'
nowrap='true'><span><xsl:value-of select=""data/Products/" + rs.Fields(x).Name  +
"""/></span></td>")
```

TEXTAREA

```
        txtstream.WriteLine("<td                              align='left'
nowrap='true'><textarea><xsl:value-of        select=""data/Products/"          +
rs.Fields(x).Name  + """/></textarea></td>")
```

TEXTBOX

```
        txtstream.WriteLine("<td         align='left'      nowrap='true'><input
type='text'><xsl:attribute name=""value""><xsl:value-of select=""data/Products/"
+ rs.Fields(x).Name  + """/></xsl:attribute></input></td>")
```

```
    txtstream.WriteLine("</tr>")
    txtstream.WriteLine("</xsl:for-each>")
```

Single Line Vertical Reports

```
    for x = 0 to rs.Fields.count-1
        txtstream.WriteLine("<tr><th>" + rs.Fields(x).Name + "</th>")
```

NONE

```
        txtstream.WriteLine("<td><xsl:value-of      select=""data/Products/"     +
rs.Fields(x).Name  + """/></td></tr>")
```

BUTTON

txtstream.WriteLine("<td align='left' nowrap='true'><button style='width:100%;'><xsl:value-of select=""data/Products/" + rs.Fields(x).Name + """/></button></td></tr>")

COMBOBOX

txtstream.WriteLine("<td align='left' nowrap='true'><select><option><xsl:attribute name='value'><xsl:value-of select=""data/Products/" + rs.Fields(x).Name + """/></xsl:attribute><xsl:value-of select=""data/Products/" + rs.Fields(x).Name + """/></option></select></td></tr>")

DIV

txtstream.WriteLine("<td align='left' nowrap='true'> <xsl:value-of select=""data/Products/" + rs.Fields(x).Name + """/> </td></tr>")

LINK

txtstream.WriteLine("<td align='left' nowrap='true'><a href='" + rs.Fields(x).Value + "'><xsl:value-of select=""data/Products/" + rs.Fields(x).Name + """/></a></td></tr>")

LISTBOX

txtstream.WriteLine("<td align='left' nowrap='true'><select multiple><option><xsl:attribute name='value'><xsl:value-of select=""data/Products/" + rs.Fields(x).Name + """/></xsl:attribute><xsl:value-of select=""data/Products/" + rs.Fields(x).Name + """/></option></select></td></tr>")

SPAN

```
        txtstream.WriteLine("<td                              align='left'
nowrap='true'><span><xsl:value-of select=""data/Products/" + rs.Fields(x).Name +
"""/></span></td></tr>")
```

TEXTAREA

```
        txtstream.WriteLine("<td                              align='left'
nowrap='true'><textarea><xsl:value-of        select=""data/Products/"          +
rs.Fields(x).Name + """/></textarea></td></tr>")
```

TEXTBOX

```
        txtstream.WriteLine("<td        align='left'     nowrap='true'><input
type='text'><xsl:attribute name=""value""><xsl:value-of select=""data/Products/"
+ rs.Fields(x).Name + """/></xsl:attribute></input></td></tr>")
```

Multi Line Vertical Reports

```
txtstream.WriteLine("<table border='0' Cellpadding='2' cellspacing='2>")
```

```
    for x = 0 to rs.Fields.count-1
        txtstream.WriteLine("<tr><th       align='left'     nowrap='true'>"      +
rs.Fields(x).Name + "</th>")
```

NONE

txtstream.WriteLine("<xsl:for-each select=""data/Products""><td align='left' nowrap='true'><xsl:value-of select=""" + rs.Fields(x).Name + """/></td></xsl:for-each></tr>")

BUTTON

txtstream.WriteLine("<xsl:for-each select=""data/Products""><td align='left' nowrap='true'><button style='width:100%;'><xsl:value-of select=""" + rs.Fields(x).Name + """/></button></td></xsl:for-each></tr>")

COMBOBOX

txtstream.WriteLine("<xsl:for-each select=""data/Products""><td align='left' nowrap='true'><select><option><xsl:attribute name='value'><xsl:value-of select=""" + rs.Fields(x).Name + """/></xsl:attribute><xsl:value-of select=""data/Products/" + rs.Fields(x).Name + """/></option></select></td></xsl:for-each></tr>")

DIV

txtstream.WriteLine("<xsl:for-each select=""data/Products""><td align='left' nowrap='true'> <xsl:value-of select=""data/Products/" + rs.Fields(x).Name + """/> </td></xsl:for-each></tr>")

LINK

txtstream.WriteLine("<xsl:for-each select=""data/Products""><td align='left' nowrap='true'><a href='" + rs.Fields(x).Value + "'><xsl:value-of select=""data/Products/" + rs.Fields(x).Name + """/></a></td></xsl:for-each></tr>")

LISTBOX

```
txtstream.WriteLine("<xsl:for-each          select=""data/Products""><td
align='left'          nowrap='true'><select          multiple><option><xsl:attribute
name='value'><xsl:value-of  select=""data/Products/"  +  rs.Fields(x).Name  +
"""/></xsl:attribute><xsl:value-of select=""data/Products/" + rs.Fields(x).Name  +
"""/></option></select></td></xsl:for-each></tr>")
```

SPAN

```
txtstream.WriteLine("<xsl:for-each          select=""data/Products""><td
align='left'   nowrap='true'><span><xsl:value-of   select=""data/Products/"   +
rs.Fields(x).Name + """/></span></td></xsl:for-each></tr>")
```

TEXTAREA

```
txtstream.WriteLine("<xsl:for-each          select=""data/Products""><td
align='left'  nowrap='true'><textarea><xsl:value-of   select=""data/Products/"   +
rs.Fields(x).Name + """/></textarea></td></xsl:for-each></tr>")
```

TEXTBOX

```
txtstream.WriteLine("<xsl:for-each          select=""data/Products""><td
align='left'          nowrap='true'><input          type='text'><xsl:attribute
name=""value""><xsl:value-of select=""data/Products/" + rs.Fields(x).Name  +
"""/></xsl:attribute></input></td></xsl:for-each></tr>")
```

Single Line Horizontal Tables

```
txtstream.WriteLine("<table    style='border:Double;border-width:1px;border-
color:navy;' rules=all frames=both cellpadding=2 cellspacing=2 Width=0>")


    txtstream.WriteLine("<tr>")
    for x = 0 to rs.Fields.count-1
        txtstream.WriteLine("<th align='left' nowrap='true'>" + rs.Fields(x).Name
+ "</th>")

    txtstream.WriteLine("</tr>")
    txtstream.WriteLine("<tr>")
    for x = 0 to rs.Fields.count-1
```

NONE

```
        txtstream.WriteLine("<td><xsl:value-of    select=""data/Products/"    +
rs.Fields(x).Name  + """/></td>")
```

BUTTON

```
        txtstream.WriteLine("<td       align='left'    nowrap='true'><button
style='width:100%;'><xsl:value-of select=""data/Products/" + rs.Fields(x).Name +
"""/></button></td>")
```

COMBOBOX

```
        txtstream.WriteLine("<td                            align='left'
nowrap='true'><select><option><xsl:attribute       name='value'><xsl:value-of
select=""data/Products/" + rs.Fields(x).Name  + """/></xsl:attribute><xsl:value-of
select=""data/Products/" + rs.Fields(x).Name  + """/></option></select></td>")
```

DIV

```
txtstream.WriteLine("<td  align='left' nowrap='true'><div><xsl:value-
of select=""data/Products/" + rs.Fields(x).Name + """/></div></td>")
```

LINK

```
txtstream.WriteLine("<td  align='left' nowrap='true'><a href='" +
rs.Fields(x).Value + "'><xsl:value-of select=""data/Products/" + rs.Fields(x).Name
+ """/></a></td>")
```

LISTBOX

```
txtstream.WriteLine("<td  align='left'  nowrap='true'><select
multiple><option><xsl:attribute  name='value'><xsl:value-of
select=""data/Products/" + rs.Fields(x).Name + """/></xsl:attribute><xsl:value-of
select=""data/Products/" + rs.Fields(x).Name + """/></option></select></td>")
```

SPAN

```
txtstream.WriteLine("<td  align='left'
nowrap='true'><span><xsl:value-of select=""data/Products/" + rs.Fields(x).Name +
"""/></span></td>")
```

TEXTAREA

```
txtstream.WriteLine("<td  align='left'
nowrap='true'><textarea><xsl:value-of  select=""data/Products/"  +
rs.Fields(x).Name + """/></textarea></td>")
```

TEXTBOX

```
        txtstream.WriteLine("<td        align='left'    nowrap='true'><input
type='text'><xsl:attribute name=""value""><xsl:value-of select=""data/Products/"
+ rs.Fields(x).Name + """/></xsl:attribute></input></td>")

        txtstream.WriteLine("</tr>")
```

Multi Line Horizontal Tables

```
        txtstream.WriteLine("<table      style='border:Double;border-width:1px;border-
color:navy;' rules=all frames=both cellpadding=2 cellspacing=2 Width=0>")


        txtstream.WriteLine("<tr>")
        for x = 0 to rs.Fields.count-1
            txtstream.WriteLine("<th>" + rs.Fields(x).Name + "</th>")

        txtstream.WriteLine("</tr>")
        txtstream.WriteLine("<xsl:for-each select=""data/Products"">")
        txtstream.WriteLine("<tr>")
        for x = 0 to rs.Fields.count-1
            txtstream.WriteLine("<td><xsl:value-of select="" " + rs.Fields(x).Name +
" ""/></td>")
```

NONE

```
        txtstream.WriteLine("<td><xsl:value-of select=""""" + rs.Fields(x).Name +
"""""/></td>")
```

BUTTON

txtstream.WriteLine("<td align='left' nowrap='true'><button style='width:100%;'><xsl:value-of select='"'" + rs.Fields(x).Name + "'"'/></button></td>")

COMBOBOX

txtstream.WriteLine("<td align='left' nowrap='true'><select><option><xsl:attribute name='value'><xsl:value-of select='"'" + rs.Fields(x).Name + "'"'/></xsl:attribute><xsl:value-of select='"data/Products/" + rs.Fields(x).Name + "'"'/></option></select></td>")

DIV

txtstream.WriteLine("<td align='left' nowrap='true'> <xsl:value-of select='"data/Products/" + rs.Fields(x).Name + "'"'/> </td>")

LINK

txtstream.WriteLine("<td align='left' nowrap='true'><a href='" + rs.Fields(x).Value + "'><xsl:value-of select='"data/Products/" + rs.Fields(x).Name + "'"'/></a></td>")

LISTBOX

txtstream.WriteLine("<td align='left' nowrap='true'><select multiple><option><xsl:attribute name='value'><xsl:value-of select='"data/Products/" + rs.Fields(x).Name + "'"'/></xsl:attribute><xsl:value-of select='"data/Products/" + rs.Fields(x).Name + "'"'/></option></select></td>")

SPAN

```
txtstream.WriteLine("<td                                    align='left'
nowrap='true'><span><xsl:value-of select=""data/Products/" + rs.Fields(x).Name +
"""/></span></td>")
```

TEXTAREA

```
txtstream.WriteLine("<td                                    align='left'
nowrap='true'><textarea><xsl:value-of        select=""data/Products/"         +
rs.Fields(x).Name + """/></textarea></td>")
```

TEXTBOX

```
txtstream.WriteLine("<td        align='left'      nowrap='true'><input
type='text'><xsl:attribute name=""value""><xsl:value-of select=""data/Products/"
+ rs.Fields(x).Name + """/></xsl:attribute></input></td>")
```

```
txtstream.WriteLine("</tr>")
txtstream.WriteLine("</xsl:for-each>")
```

Single Line Vertical Tables

```
for x = 0 to rs.Fields.count-1
    txtstream.WriteLine("<tr><th>" + rs.Fields(x).Name + "</th>")
```

NONE

```
txtstream.WriteLine("<td><xsl:value-of      select=""data/Products/"      +
rs.Fields(x).Name + """/></td></tr>")
```

BUTTON

txtstream.WriteLine("<td   align='left'   nowrap='true'><button style='width:100%;'><xsl:value-of select=""data/Products/" + rs.Fields(x).Name + """/></button></td></tr>")

COMBOBOX

txtstream.WriteLine("<td   align='left' nowrap='true'><select><option><xsl:attribute   name='value'><xsl:value-of select=""data/Products/" + rs.Fields(x).Name + """/></xsl:attribute><xsl:value-of select=""data/Products/"   +   rs.Fields(x).Name   + """/></option></select></td></tr>")

DIV

txtstream.WriteLine("<td   align='left' nowrap='true'> <xsl:value-of select=""data/Products/" + rs.Fields(x).Name + """/> </td></tr>")

LINK

txtstream.WriteLine("<td   align='left' nowrap='true'><a href='" + rs.Fields(x).Value + "'><xsl:value-of select=""data/Products/" + rs.Fields(x).Name + """/></a></td></tr>")

LISTBOX

txtstream.WriteLine("<td   align='left'   nowrap='true'><select multiple><option><xsl:attribute   name='value'><xsl:value-of select=""data/Products/" + rs.Fields(x).Name + """/></xsl:attribute><xsl:value-of select=""data/Products/"   +   rs.Fields(x).Name   + """/></option></select></td></tr>")

SPAN

```
txtstream.WriteLine("<td                                              align='left'
nowrap='true'><span><xsl:value-of select=""data/Products/" + rs.Fields(x).Name +
"""/></span></td></tr>")
```

TEXTAREA

```
txtstream.WriteLine("<td                                              align='left'
nowrap='true'><textarea><xsl:value-of        select=""data/Products/"         +
rs.Fields(x).Name + """/></textarea></td></tr>")
```

TEXTBOX

```
txtstream.WriteLine("<td          align='left'     nowrap='true'><input
type='text'><xsl:attribute name=""value""><xsl:value-of select=""data/Products/"
+ rs.Fields(x).Name + """/></xsl:attribute></input></td></tr>")
```

Multi Line Vertical Tables

```
txtstream.WriteLine("<table     style='border:Double;border-width:1px;border-
color:navy;' rules=all frames=both cellpadding=2 cellspacing=2 Width=0>")


for x = 0 to rs.Fields.count-1
        txtstream.WriteLine("<tr><th       align='left'     nowrap='true'>"     +
rs.Fields(x).Name + "</th>")
```

NONE

```
txtstream.WriteLine("<xsl:for-each        select=""data/Products""><td
align='left'  nowrap='true'><xsl:value-of  select="""  +  rs.Fields(x).Name     +
"""/></td></xsl:for-each></tr>")
```

BUTTON

txtstream.WriteLine("<xsl:for-each select=""data/Products""><td align='left' nowrap='true'><button style='width:100%;'><xsl:value-of select=""" + rs.Fields(x).Name + """/></button></td></xsl:for-each></tr>")

COMBOBOX

txtstream.WriteLine("<xsl:for-each select=""data/Products""><td align='left' nowrap='true'><select><option><xsl:attribute name='value'><xsl:value-of select=""" + rs.Fields(x).Name + """/></xsl:attribute><xsl:value-of select=""data/Products/" + rs.Fields(x).Name + """/></option></select></td></xsl:for-each></tr>")

DIV

txtstream.WriteLine("<xsl:for-each select=""data/Products""><td align='left' nowrap='true'> <xsl:value-of select=""data/Products/" + rs.Fields(x).Name + """/> </td></xsl:for-each></tr>")

LINK

txtstream.WriteLine("<xsl:for-each select=""data/Products""><td align='left' nowrap='true'><a href='" + rs.Fields(x).Value + "'><xsl:value-of select=""data/Products/" + rs.Fields(x).Name + """/></a></td></xsl:for-each></tr>")

LISTBOX

```
txtstream.WriteLine("<xsl:for-each    select=""data/Products"">"><td
align='left'        nowrap='true'><select         multiple><option><xsl:attribute
name='value'><xsl:value-of  select=""data/Products/" + rs.Fields(x).Name +
"""/></xsl:attribute><xsl:value-of select=""data/Products/" + rs.Fields(x).Name +
"""/></option></select></td></xsl:for-each></tr>")
```

SPAN

```
txtstream.WriteLine("<xsl:for-each    select=""data/Products"">"><td
align='left'    nowrap='true'><span><xsl:value-of    select=""data/Products/"   +
rs.Fields(x).Name + """/></span></td></xsl:for-each></tr>")
```

TEXTAREA

```
txtstream.WriteLine("<xsl:for-each    select=""data/Products"">"><td
align='left'   nowrap='true'><textarea><xsl:value-of  select=""data/Products/"   +
rs.Fields(x).Name + """/></textarea></td></xsl:for-each></tr>")
```

TEXTBOX

```
txtstream.WriteLine("<xsl:for-each    select=""data/Products"">"><td
align='left'            nowrap='true'><input          type='text'><xsl:attribute
name=""value""><xsl:value-of  select=""data/Products/" + rs.Fields(x).Name +
"""/></xsl:attribute></input></td></xsl:for-each></tr>")
```

```
txtstream.WriteLine("</table>")
txtstream.WriteLine("</body>")
txtstream.WriteLine("</html>")
```

```
txtstream.WriteLine("</xsl:template>")
txtstream.WriteLine("</xsl:stylesheet>")
txtstream.Close()
```

Stylesheets

Add some Pizzazz To your ASP, HTA, HTML and

XSL pages

ELOW is an assortment of stylesheets. There is nothing spectacular about them Just some ideas you can modify and put your own twist on them.

None

```
txtstream.WriteLine("<style type='text/css'>")
txtstream.WriteLine("th")
txtstream.WriteLine("{")
txtstream.WriteLine("   COLOR: Black;")
txtstream.WriteLine("}")
txtstream.WriteLine("td")
txtstream.WriteLine("{")
txtstream.WriteLine("   COLOR: Black;")
txtstream.WriteLine("}")
txtstream.WriteLine("</style>")
```

Its A Table

```
txtstream.WriteLine("<style type='text/css'>")
txtstream.WriteLine("#itsthetable {")
txtstream.WriteLine("      font-family: Georgia, ""Times New Roman"",
Times, serif;")
txtstream.WriteLine("      color: #036;")
```

```
txtstream.WriteLine("}")
txtstream.WriteLine("caption {")
txtstream.WriteLine("        font-size: 48px;")
txtstream.WriteLine("        color: #036;")
txtstream.WriteLine("        font-weight: bolder;")
txtstream.WriteLine("        font-variant: small-caps;")
txtstream.WriteLine("}")
txtstream.WriteLine("th {")
txtstream.WriteLine("        font-size: 12px;")
txtstream.WriteLine("        color: #FFF;")
txtstream.WriteLine("        background-color: #06C;")
txtstream.WriteLine("        padding: 8px 4px;")
txtstream.WriteLine("        border-bottom: 1px solid #015ebc;")
txtstream.WriteLine("}")
txtstream.WriteLine("table {")
txtstream.WriteLine("        margin: 0;")
txtstream.WriteLine("        padding: 0;")
txtstream.WriteLine("        border-collapse: collapse;")
txtstream.WriteLine("        border: 1px solid #06C;")
txtstream.WriteLine("        width: 100%")
txtstream.WriteLine("}")
txtstream.WriteLine("#itsthetable th a:link, #itsthetable th a:visited {")
txtstream.WriteLine("        color: #FFF;")
txtstream.WriteLine("        text-decoration: none;")
txtstream.WriteLine("        border-left: 5px solid #FFF;")
txtstream.WriteLine("        padding-left: 3px;")
txtstream.WriteLine("}")
txtstream.WriteLine("th a:hover, #itsthetable th a:active {")
txtstream.WriteLine("        color: #F90;")
txtstream.WriteLine("        text-decoration: line-through;")
txtstream.WriteLine("        border-left: 5px solid #F90;")
txtstream.WriteLine("        padding-left: 3px;")
txtstream.WriteLine("}")
```

```
txtstream.WriteLine("tbody th:hover {")
txtstream.WriteLine("        background-image:
url(imgs/tbody_hover.gif);")
txtstream.WriteLine("        background-position: bottom;")
txtstream.WriteLine("        background-repeat: repeat-x;")
txtstream.WriteLine("}")
txtstream.WriteLine("td {")
txtstream.WriteLine("        background-color: #f2f2f2;")
txtstream.WriteLine("        padding: 4px;")
txtstream.WriteLine("        font-size: 12px;")
txtstream.WriteLine("}")
txtstream.WriteLine("#itsthetable td:hover {")
txtstream.WriteLine("        background-color: #f8f8f8;")
txtstream.WriteLine("}")
txtstream.WriteLine("#itsthetable td a:link, #itsthetable td a:visited {")
txtstream.WriteLine("        color: #039;")
txtstream.WriteLine("        text-decoration: none;")
txtstream.WriteLine("        border-left: 3px solid #039;")
txtstream.WriteLine("        padding-left: 3px;")
txtstream.WriteLine("}")
txtstream.WriteLine("#itsthetable td a:hover, #itsthetable td a:active {")
txtstream.WriteLine("        color: #06C;")
txtstream.WriteLine("        text-decoration: line-through;")
txtstream.WriteLine("        border-left: 3px solid #06C;")
txtstream.WriteLine("        padding-left: 3px;")
txtstream.WriteLine("}")
txtstream.WriteLine("#itsthetable th {")
txtstream.WriteLine("        text-align: left;")
txtstream.WriteLine("        width: 150px;")
txtstream.WriteLine("}")
txtstream.WriteLine("#itsthetable tr {")
txtstream.WriteLine("        border-bottom: 1px solid #CCC;")
txtstream.WriteLine("}")
```

```
txtstream.WriteLine("#itsthetable thead th {")
txtstream.WriteLine("        background-image: url(imgs/thead_back.gif);")
txtstream.WriteLine("        background-repeat: repeat-x;")
txtstream.WriteLine("        background-color: #06C;")
txtstream.WriteLine("        height: 30px;")
txtstream.WriteLine("        font-size: 18px;")
txtstream.WriteLine("        text-align: center;")
txtstream.WriteLine("        text-shadow: #333 2px 2px;")
txtstream.WriteLine("        border: 2px;")
txtstream.WriteLine("}")
txtstream.WriteLine("#itsthetable tfoot th {")
txtstream.WriteLine("        background-image: url(imgs/tfoot_back.gif);")
txtstream.WriteLine("        background-repeat: repeat-x;")
txtstream.WriteLine("        background-color: #036;")
txtstream.WriteLine("        height: 30px;")
txtstream.WriteLine("        font-size: 28px;")
txtstream.WriteLine("        text-align: center;")
txtstream.WriteLine("        text-shadow: #333 2px 2px;")
txtstream.WriteLine("}")
txtstream.WriteLine("#itsthetable tfoot td {")
txtstream.WriteLine("        background-image: url(imgs/tfoot_back.gif);")
txtstream.WriteLine("        background-repeat: repeat-x;")
txtstream.WriteLine("        background-color: #036;")
txtstream.WriteLine("        color: FFF;")
txtstream.WriteLine("        height: 30px;")
txtstream.WriteLine("        font-size: 24px;")
txtstream.WriteLine("        text-align: left;")
txtstream.WriteLine("        text-shadow: #333 2px 2px;")
txtstream.WriteLine("}")
txtstream.WriteLine("tbody td a[href=""http://www.csslab.cl/""] {")
txtstream.WriteLine("        font-weight: bolder;")
txtstream.WriteLine("}")
txtstream.WriteLine("</style>")
```

Black and White Text

```
txtstream.WriteLine("<style type='text/css'>")
txtstream.WriteLine("th")
txtstream.WriteLine("{")
txtstream.WriteLine("    COLOR: white;")
txtstream.WriteLine("    BACKGROUND-COLOR: black;")
txtstream.WriteLine("    FONT-FAMILY:font-family: Cambria, serif;")
txtstream.WriteLine("    FONT-SIZE: 12px;")
txtstream.WriteLine("    text-align: left;")
txtstream.WriteLine("    white-Space: nowrap='nowrap';")
txtstream.WriteLine("}")
txtstream.WriteLine("td")
txtstream.WriteLine("{")
txtstream.WriteLine("    COLOR: white;")
txtstream.WriteLine("    BACKGROUND-COLOR: black;")
txtstream.WriteLine("    FONT-FAMILY: font-family: Cambria, serif;")
txtstream.WriteLine("    FONT-SIZE: 12px;")
txtstream.WriteLine("    text-align: left;")
txtstream.WriteLine("    white-Space: nowrap='nowrap';")
txtstream.WriteLine("}")
txtstream.WriteLine("div")
txtstream.WriteLine("{")
txtstream.WriteLine("    COLOR: white;")
txtstream.WriteLine("    BACKGROUND-COLOR: black;")
txtstream.WriteLine("    FONT-FAMILY: font-family: Cambria, serif;")
txtstream.WriteLine("    FONT-SIZE: 10px;")
txtstream.WriteLine("    text-align: left;")
txtstream.WriteLine("    white-Space: nowrap='nowrap';")
txtstream.WriteLine("}")
txtstream.WriteLine("span")
txtstream.WriteLine("{")
```

```
txtstream.WriteLine("   COLOR: white;")
txtstream.WriteLine("   BACKGROUND-COLOR: black;")
txtstream.WriteLine("   FONT-FAMILY: font-family: Cambria, serif;")
txtstream.WriteLine("   FONT-SIZE: 10px;")
txtstream.WriteLine("   text-align: left;")
txtstream.WriteLine("   white-Space: nowrap='nowrap';")
txtstream.WriteLine("   display:inline-block;")
txtstream.WriteLine("   width: 100%;")
txtstream.WriteLine("}")
txtstream.WriteLine("textarea")
txtstream.WriteLine("{")
txtstream.WriteLine("   COLOR: white;")
txtstream.WriteLine("   BACKGROUND-COLOR: black;")
txtstream.WriteLine("   FONT-FAMILY: font-family: Cambria, serif;")
txtstream.WriteLine("   FONT-SIZE: 10px;")
txtstream.WriteLine("   text-align: left;")
txtstream.WriteLine("   white-Space: nowrap='nowrap';")
txtstream.WriteLine("   width: 100%;")
txtstream.WriteLine("}")
txtstream.WriteLine("select")
txtstream.WriteLine("{")
txtstream.WriteLine("   COLOR: white;")
txtstream.WriteLine("   BACKGROUND-COLOR: black;")
txtstream.WriteLine("   FONT-FAMILY: font-family: Cambria, serif;")
txtstream.WriteLine("   FONT-SIZE: 10px;")
txtstream.WriteLine("   text-align: left;")
txtstream.WriteLine("   white-Space: nowrap='nowrap';")
txtstream.WriteLine("   width: 100%;")
txtstream.WriteLine("}")
txtstream.WriteLine("input")
txtstream.WriteLine("{")
txtstream.WriteLine("   COLOR: white;")
txtstream.WriteLine("   BACKGROUND-COLOR: black;")
```

```
txtstream.WriteLine("   FONT-FAMILY: font-family: Cambria, serif;")
txtstream.WriteLine("   FONT-SIZE: 12px;")
txtstream.WriteLine("   text-align: left;")
txtstream.WriteLine("   display:table-cell;")
txtstream.WriteLine("   white-Space: nowrap='nowrap';")
txtstream.WriteLine("}")
txtstream.WriteLine("h1 {")
txtstream.WriteLine("color: antiquewhite;")
txtstream.WriteLine("text-shadow: 1px 1px 1px black;")
txtstream.WriteLine("padding: 3px;")
txtstream.WriteLine("text-align: center;")
txtstream.WriteLine("box-shadow: in2px 2px 5px rgba(0,0,0,0.5), in-2px -
2px 5px rgba(255,255,255,0.5);")
txtstream.WriteLine("}")
txtstream.WriteLine("</style>")
```

Colored Text

```
txtstream.WriteLine("<style type='text/css'>")
txtstream.WriteLine("th")
txtstream.WriteLine("{")
txtstream.WriteLine("   COLOR: darkred;")
txtstream.WriteLine("   BACKGROUND-COLOR: #eeeeee;")
txtstream.WriteLine("   FONT-FAMILY:font-family: Cambria, serif;")
txtstream.WriteLine("   FONT-SIZE: 12px;")
txtstream.WriteLine("   text-align: left;")
txtstream.WriteLine("   white-Space: nowrap='nowrap';")
txtstream.WriteLine("}")
txtstream.WriteLine("td")
txtstream.WriteLine("{")
txtstream.WriteLine("   COLOR: navy;")
txtstream.WriteLine("   BACKGROUND-COLOR: #eeeeee;")
txtstream.WriteLine("   FONT-FAMILY: font-family: Cambria, serif;")
```

```
txtstream.WriteLine("    FONT-SIZE: 12px;")
txtstream.WriteLine("    text-align: left;")
txtstream.WriteLine("    white-Space: nowrap='nowrap';")
txtstream.WriteLine("}")
txtstream.WriteLine("div")
txtstream.WriteLine("{")
txtstream.WriteLine("    COLOR: white;")
txtstream.WriteLine("    BACKGROUND-COLOR: navy;")
txtstream.WriteLine("    FONT-FAMILY: font-family: Cambria, serif;")
txtstream.WriteLine("    FONT-SIZE: 10px;")
txtstream.WriteLine("    text-align: left;")
txtstream.WriteLine("    white-Space: nowrap='nowrap';")
txtstream.WriteLine("}")
txtstream.WriteLine("span")
txtstream.WriteLine("{")
txtstream.WriteLine("    COLOR: white;")
txtstream.WriteLine("    BACKGROUND-COLOR: navy;")
txtstream.WriteLine("    FONT-FAMILY: font-family: Cambria, serif;")
txtstream.WriteLine("    FONT-SIZE: 10px;")
txtstream.WriteLine("    text-align: left;")
txtstream.WriteLine("    white-Space: nowrap='nowrap';")
txtstream.WriteLine("    display:inline-block;")
txtstream.WriteLine("    width: 100%;")
txtstream.WriteLine("}")
txtstream.WriteLine("textarea")
txtstream.WriteLine("{")
txtstream.WriteLine("    COLOR: white;")
txtstream.WriteLine("    BACKGROUND-COLOR: navy;")
txtstream.WriteLine("    FONT-FAMILY: font-family: Cambria, serif;")
txtstream.WriteLine("    FONT-SIZE: 10px;")
txtstream.WriteLine("    text-align: left;")
txtstream.WriteLine("    white-Space: nowrap='nowrap';")
txtstream.WriteLine("    width: 100%;")
```

```
txtstream.WriteLine("}")
txtstream.WriteLine("select")
txtstream.WriteLine("{")
txtstream.WriteLine("   COLOR: white;")
txtstream.WriteLine("   BACKGROUND-COLOR: navy;")
txtstream.WriteLine("   FONT-FAMILY: font-family: Cambria, serif;")
txtstream.WriteLine("   FONT-SIZE: 10px;")
txtstream.WriteLine("   text-align: left;")
txtstream.WriteLine("   white-Space: nowrap='nowrap';")
txtstream.WriteLine("   width: 100%;")
txtstream.WriteLine("}")
txtstream.WriteLine("input")
txtstream.WriteLine("{")
txtstream.WriteLine("   COLOR: white;")
txtstream.WriteLine("   BACKGROUND-COLOR: navy;")
txtstream.WriteLine("   FONT-FAMILY: font-family: Cambria, serif;")
txtstream.WriteLine("   FONT-SIZE: 12px;")
txtstream.WriteLine("   text-align: left;")
txtstream.WriteLine("   display:table-cell;")
txtstream.WriteLine("   white-Space: nowrap='nowrap';")
txtstream.WriteLine("}")
txtstream.WriteLine("h1 {")
txtstream.WriteLine("color: antiquewhite;")
txtstream.WriteLine("text-shadow: 1px 1px 1px black;")
txtstream.WriteLine("padding: 3px;")
txtstream.WriteLine("text-align: center;")
txtstream.WriteLine("box-shadow: in2px 2px 5px rgba(0,0,0,0.5), in-2px -2px 5px rgba(255,255,255,0.5);")
txtstream.WriteLine("}")
txtstream.WriteLine("</style>")
```

Oscillating Row Colors

```
txtstream.WriteLine("<style type='text/css'>")
txtstream.WriteLine("th")
txtstream.WriteLine("{")
txtstream.WriteLine("    COLOR: white;")
txtstream.WriteLine("    BACKGROUND-COLOR: navy;")
txtstream.WriteLine("    FONT-FAMILY:font-family: Cambria, serif;")
txtstream.WriteLine("    FONT-SIZE: 12px;")
txtstream.WriteLine("    text-align: left;")
txtstream.WriteLine("    white-Space: nowrap='nowrap';")
txtstream.WriteLine("}")
txtstream.WriteLine("td")
txtstream.WriteLine("{")
txtstream.WriteLine("    COLOR: navy;")
txtstream.WriteLine("    FONT-FAMILY: font-family: Cambria, serif;")
txtstream.WriteLine("    FONT-SIZE: 12px;")
txtstream.WriteLine("    text-align: left;")
txtstream.WriteLine("    white-Space: nowrap='nowrap';")
txtstream.WriteLine("}")
txtstream.WriteLine("div")
txtstream.WriteLine("{")
txtstream.WriteLine("    COLOR: navy;")
txtstream.WriteLine("    FONT-FAMILY: font-family: Cambria, serif;")
txtstream.WriteLine("    FONT-SIZE: 12px;")
txtstream.WriteLine("    text-align: left;")
txtstream.WriteLine("    white-Space: nowrap='nowrap';")
txtstream.WriteLine("}")
txtstream.WriteLine("span")
txtstream.WriteLine("{")
txtstream.WriteLine("    COLOR: navy;")
txtstream.WriteLine("    FONT-FAMILY: font-family: Cambria, serif;")
txtstream.WriteLine("    FONT-SIZE: 12px;")
txtstream.WriteLine("    text-align: left;")
txtstream.WriteLine("    white-Space: nowrap='nowrap';")
```

```
txtstream.WriteLine("    width: 100%;")
txtstream.WriteLine("}")
txtstream.WriteLine("textarea")
txtstream.WriteLine("{")
txtstream.WriteLine("    COLOR: navy;")
txtstream.WriteLine("    FONT-FAMILY: font-family: Cambria, serif;")
txtstream.WriteLine("    FONT-SIZE: 12px;")
txtstream.WriteLine("    text-align: left;")
txtstream.WriteLine("    white-Space: nowrap='nowrap';")
txtstream.WriteLine("    display:inline-block;")
txtstream.WriteLine("    width: 100%;")
txtstream.WriteLine("}")
txtstream.WriteLine("select")
txtstream.WriteLine("{")
txtstream.WriteLine("    COLOR: navy;")
txtstream.WriteLine("    FONT-FAMILY: font-family: Cambria, serif;")
txtstream.WriteLine("    FONT-SIZE: 10px;")
txtstream.WriteLine("    text-align: left;")
txtstream.WriteLine("    white-Space: nowrap='nowrap';")
txtstream.WriteLine("    display:inline-block;")
txtstream.WriteLine("    width: 100%;")
txtstream.WriteLine("}")
txtstream.WriteLine("input")
txtstream.WriteLine("{")
txtstream.WriteLine("    COLOR: navy;")
txtstream.WriteLine("    FONT-FAMILY: font-family: Cambria, serif;")
txtstream.WriteLine("    FONT-SIZE: 12px;")
txtstream.WriteLine("    text-align: left;")
txtstream.WriteLine("    display:table-cell;")
txtstream.WriteLine("    white-Space: nowrap='nowrap';")
txtstream.WriteLine("}")
txtstream.WriteLine("h1 {")
txtstream.WriteLine("color: antiquewhite;")
```

```
txtstream.WriteLine("text-shadow: 1px 1px 1px black;")
txtstream.WriteLine("padding: 3px;")
txtstream.WriteLine("text-align: center;")
txtstream.WriteLine("box-shadow: in2px 2px 5px rgba(0,0,0,0.5), in-2px -
2px 5px rgba(255,255,255,0.5);")
txtstream.WriteLine("}")
txtstream.WriteLine("tr:nth-child(even){background-color:#f2f2f2;}")
txtstream.WriteLine("tr:nth-child(odd){background-color:#cccccc;
color:#f2f2f2;}")
txtstream.WriteLine("</style>")
```

Ghost Decorated

```
txtstream.WriteLine("<style type='text/css'>")
txtstream.WriteLine("th")
txtstream.WriteLine("{")
txtstream.WriteLine("   COLOR: black;")
txtstream.WriteLine("   BACKGROUND-COLOR: white;")
txtstream.WriteLine("   FONT-FAMILY:font-family: Cambria, serif;")
txtstream.WriteLine("   FONT-SIZE: 12px;")
txtstream.WriteLine("   text-align: left;")
txtstream.WriteLine("   white-Space: nowrap='nowrap';")
txtstream.WriteLine("}")
txtstream.WriteLine("td")
txtstream.WriteLine("{")
txtstream.WriteLine("   COLOR: black;")
txtstream.WriteLine("   BACKGROUND-COLOR: white;")
txtstream.WriteLine("   FONT-FAMILY: font-family: Cambria, serif;")
txtstream.WriteLine("   FONT-SIZE: 12px;")
txtstream.WriteLine("   text-align: left;")
txtstream.WriteLine("   white-Space: nowrap='nowrap';")
txtstream.WriteLine("}")
txtstream.WriteLine("div")
```

```
txtstream.WriteLine("{")
txtstream.WriteLine("   COLOR: black;")
txtstream.WriteLine("   BACKGROUND-COLOR: white;")
txtstream.WriteLine("   FONT-FAMILY: font-family: Cambria, serif;")
txtstream.WriteLine("   FONT-SIZE: 10px;")
txtstream.WriteLine("   text-align: left;")
txtstream.WriteLine("   white-Space: nowrap='nowrap';")
txtstream.WriteLine("}")
txtstream.WriteLine("span")
txtstream.WriteLine("{")
txtstream.WriteLine("   COLOR: black;")
txtstream.WriteLine("   BACKGROUND-COLOR: white;")
txtstream.WriteLine("   FONT-FAMILY: font-family: Cambria, serif;")
txtstream.WriteLine("   FONT-SIZE: 10px;")
txtstream.WriteLine("   text-align: left;")
txtstream.WriteLine("   white-Space: nowrap='nowrap';")
txtstream.WriteLine("   display:inline-block;")
txtstream.WriteLine("   width: 100%;")
txtstream.WriteLine("}")
txtstream.WriteLine("textarea")
txtstream.WriteLine("{")
txtstream.WriteLine("   COLOR: black;")
txtstream.WriteLine("   BACKGROUND-COLOR: white;")
txtstream.WriteLine("   FONT-FAMILY: font-family: Cambria, serif;")
txtstream.WriteLine("   FONT-SIZE: 10px;")
txtstream.WriteLine("   text-align: left;")
txtstream.WriteLine("   white-Space: nowrap='nowrap';")
txtstream.WriteLine("   width: 100%;")
txtstream.WriteLine("}")
txtstream.WriteLine("select")
txtstream.WriteLine("{")
txtstream.WriteLine("   COLOR: black;")
txtstream.WriteLine("   BACKGROUND-COLOR: white;")
```

```
txtstream.WriteLine("   FONT-FAMILY: font-family: Cambria, serif;")
txtstream.WriteLine("   FONT-SIZE: 10px;")
txtstream.WriteLine("   text-align: left;")
txtstream.WriteLine("   white-Space: nowrap='nowrap';")
txtstream.WriteLine("   width: 100%;")
txtstream.WriteLine("}")
txtstream.WriteLine("input")
txtstream.WriteLine("{")
txtstream.WriteLine("   COLOR: black;")
txtstream.WriteLine("   BACKGROUND-COLOR: white;")
txtstream.WriteLine("   FONT-FAMILY: font-family: Cambria, serif;")
txtstream.WriteLine("   FONT-SIZE: 12px;")
txtstream.WriteLine("   text-align: left;")
txtstream.WriteLine("   display:table-cell;")
txtstream.WriteLine("   white-Space: nowrap='nowrap';")
txtstream.WriteLine("}")
txtstream.WriteLine("h1 {")
txtstream.WriteLine("color: antiquewhite;")
txtstream.WriteLine("text-shadow: 1px 1px 1px black;")
txtstream.WriteLine("padding: 3px;")
txtstream.WriteLine("text-align: center;")
txtstream.WriteLine("box-shadow: in2px 2px 5px rgba(0,0,0,0.5), in-2px -2px 5px rgba(255,255,255,0.5);")
txtstream.WriteLine("}")
txtstream.WriteLine("</style>")
```

3D

```
txtstream.WriteLine("<style type='text/css'>")
txtstream.WriteLine("body")
txtstream.WriteLine("{")
txtstream.WriteLine("   PADDING-RIGHT: 0px;")
txtstream.WriteLine("   PADDING-LEFT: 0px;")
```

```
txtstream.WriteLine("    PADDING-BOTTOM: 0px;")
txtstream.WriteLine("    MARGIN: 0px;")
txtstream.WriteLine("    COLOR: #333;")
txtstream.WriteLine("    PADDING-TOP: 0px;")
txtstream.WriteLine("        FONT-FAMILY: verdana, arial, helvetica, sans-
serif;")
txtstream.WriteLine("}")
txtstream.WriteLine("table")
txtstream.WriteLine("{")
txtstream.WriteLine("    BORDER-RIGHT: #999999 3px solid;")
txtstream.WriteLine("    PADDING-RIGHT: 6px;")
txtstream.WriteLine("    PADDING-LEFT: 6px;")
txtstream.WriteLine("    FONT-WEIGHT: Bold;")
txtstream.WriteLine("    FONT-SIZE: 14px;")
txtstream.WriteLine("    PADDING-BOTTOM: 6px;")
txtstream.WriteLine("    COLOR: Peru;")
txtstream.WriteLine("    LINE-HEIGHT: 14px;")
txtstream.WriteLine("    PADDING-TOP: 6px;")
txtstream.WriteLine("    BORDER-BOTTOM: #999 1px solid;")
txtstream.WriteLine("    BACKGROUND-COLOR: #eeeeee;")
txtstream.WriteLine("        FONT-FAMILY: verdana, arial, helvetica, sans-
serif;")
txtstream.WriteLine("    FONT-SIZE: 12px;")
txtstream.WriteLine("}")
txtstream.WriteLine("th")
txtstream.WriteLine("{")
txtstream.WriteLine("    BORDER-RIGHT: #999999 3px solid;")
txtstream.WriteLine("    PADDING-RIGHT: 6px;")
txtstream.WriteLine("    PADDING-LEFT: 6px;")
txtstream.WriteLine("    FONT-WEIGHT: Bold;")
txtstream.WriteLine("    FONT-SIZE: 14px;")
txtstream.WriteLine("    PADDING-BOTTOM: 6px;")
txtstream.WriteLine("    COLOR: darkred;")
```

```
txtstream.WriteLine("    LINE-HEIGHT: 14px;")
txtstream.WriteLine("    PADDING-TOP: 6px;")
txtstream.WriteLine("    BORDER-BOTTOM: #999 1px solid;")
txtstream.WriteLine("    BACKGROUND-COLOR: #eeeeee;")
txtstream.WriteLine("    FONT-FAMILY:font-family: Cambria, serif;")
txtstream.WriteLine("    FONT-SIZE: 12px;")
txtstream.WriteLine("    text-align: left;")
txtstream.WriteLine("    white-Space: nowrap='nowrap';")
txtstream.WriteLine("}")
txtstream.WriteLine(".th")
txtstream.WriteLine("{")
txtstream.WriteLine("    BORDER-RIGHT: #999999 2px solid;")
txtstream.WriteLine("    PADDING-RIGHT: 6px;")
txtstream.WriteLine("    PADDING-LEFT: 6px;")
txtstream.WriteLine("    FONT-WEIGHT: Bold;")
txtstream.WriteLine("    PADDING-BOTTOM: 6px;")
txtstream.WriteLine("    COLOR: black;")
txtstream.WriteLine("    PADDING-TOP: 6px;")
txtstream.WriteLine("    BORDER-BOTTOM: #999 2px solid;")
txtstream.WriteLine("    BACKGROUND-COLOR: #eeeeee;")
txtstream.WriteLine("    FONT-FAMILY: font-family: Cambria, serif;")
txtstream.WriteLine("    FONT-SIZE: 10px;")
txtstream.WriteLine("    text-align: right;")
txtstream.WriteLine("    white-Space: nowrap='nowrap';")
txtstream.WriteLine("}")
txtstream.WriteLine("td")
txtstream.WriteLine("{")
txtstream.WriteLine("    BORDER-RIGHT: #999999 3px solid;")
txtstream.WriteLine("    PADDING-RIGHT: 6px;")
txtstream.WriteLine("    PADDING-LEFT: 6px;")
txtstream.WriteLine("    FONT-WEIGHT: Normal;")
txtstream.WriteLine("    PADDING-BOTTOM: 6px;")
txtstream.WriteLine("    COLOR: navy;")
```

```
txtstream.WriteLine("    LINE-HEIGHT: 14px;")
txtstream.WriteLine("    PADDING-TOP: 6px;")
txtstream.WriteLine("    BORDER-BOTTOM: #999 1px solid;")
txtstream.WriteLine("    BACKGROUND-COLOR: #eeeeee;")
txtstream.WriteLine("    FONT-FAMILY: font-family: Cambria, serif;")
txtstream.WriteLine("    FONT-SIZE: 12px;")
txtstream.WriteLine("    text-align: left;")
txtstream.WriteLine("    white-Space: nowrap='nowrap';")
txtstream.WriteLine("}")
txtstream.WriteLine("div")
txtstream.WriteLine("{")
txtstream.WriteLine("    BORDER-RIGHT: #999999 3px solid;")
txtstream.WriteLine("    PADDING-RIGHT: 6px;")
txtstream.WriteLine("    PADDING-LEFT: 6px;")
txtstream.WriteLine("    FONT-WEIGHT: Normal;")
txtstream.WriteLine("    PADDING-BOTTOM: 6px;")
txtstream.WriteLine("    COLOR: white;")
txtstream.WriteLine("    PADDING-TOP: 6px;")
txtstream.WriteLine("    BORDER-BOTTOM: #999 1px solid;")
txtstream.WriteLine("    BACKGROUND-COLOR: navy;")
txtstream.WriteLine("    FONT-FAMILY: font-family: Cambria, serif;")
txtstream.WriteLine("    FONT-SIZE: 10px;")
txtstream.WriteLine("    text-align: left;")
txtstream.WriteLine("    white-Space: nowrap='nowrap';")
txtstream.WriteLine("}")
txtstream.WriteLine("span")
txtstream.WriteLine("{")
txtstream.WriteLine("    BORDER-RIGHT: #999999 3px solid;")
txtstream.WriteLine("    PADDING-RIGHT: 3px;")
txtstream.WriteLine("    PADDING-LEFT: 3px;")
txtstream.WriteLine("    FONT-WEIGHT: Normal;")
txtstream.WriteLine("    PADDING-BOTTOM: 3px;")
txtstream.WriteLine("    COLOR: white;")
```

```
txtstream.WriteLine("    PADDING-TOP: 3px;")
txtstream.WriteLine("    BORDER-BOTTOM: #999 1px solid;")
txtstream.WriteLine("    BACKGROUND-COLOR: navy;")
txtstream.WriteLine("    FONT-FAMILY: font-family: Cambria, serif;")
txtstream.WriteLine("    FONT-SIZE: 10px;")
txtstream.WriteLine("    text-align: left;")
txtstream.WriteLine("    white-Space: nowrap='nowrap';")
txtstream.WriteLine("    display:inline-block;")
txtstream.WriteLine("    width: 100%;")
txtstream.WriteLine("}")
txtstream.WriteLine("textarea")
txtstream.WriteLine("{")
txtstream.WriteLine("    BORDER-RIGHT: #999999 3px solid;")
txtstream.WriteLine("    PADDING-RIGHT: 3px;")
txtstream.WriteLine("    PADDING-LEFT: 3px;")
txtstream.WriteLine("    FONT-WEIGHT: Normal;")
txtstream.WriteLine("    PADDING-BOTTOM: 3px;")
txtstream.WriteLine("    COLOR: white;")
txtstream.WriteLine("    PADDING-TOP: 3px;")
txtstream.WriteLine("    BORDER-BOTTOM: #999 1px solid;")
txtstream.WriteLine("    BACKGROUND-COLOR: navy;")
txtstream.WriteLine("    FONT-FAMILY: font-family: Cambria, serif;")
txtstream.WriteLine("    FONT-SIZE: 10px;")
txtstream.WriteLine("    text-align: left;")
txtstream.WriteLine("    white-Space: nowrap='nowrap';")
txtstream.WriteLine("    width: 100%;")
txtstream.WriteLine("}")
txtstream.WriteLine("select")
txtstream.WriteLine("{")
txtstream.WriteLine("    BORDER-RIGHT: #999999 3px solid;")
txtstream.WriteLine("    PADDING-RIGHT: 6px;")
txtstream.WriteLine("    PADDING-LEFT: 6px;")
txtstream.WriteLine("    FONT-WEIGHT: Normal;")
```

```
txtstream.WriteLine("    PADDING-BOTTOM: 6px;")
txtstream.WriteLine("    COLOR: white;")
txtstream.WriteLine("    PADDING-TOP: 6px;")
txtstream.WriteLine("    BORDER-BOTTOM: #999 1px solid;")
txtstream.WriteLine("    BACKGROUND-COLOR: navy;")
txtstream.WriteLine("    FONT-FAMILY: font-family: Cambria, serif;")
txtstream.WriteLine("    FONT-SIZE: 10px;")
txtstream.WriteLine("    text-align: left;")
txtstream.WriteLine("    white-Space: nowrap='nowrap';")
txtstream.WriteLine("    width: 100%;")
txtstream.WriteLine("}")
txtstream.WriteLine("input")
txtstream.WriteLine("{")
txtstream.WriteLine("    BORDER-RIGHT: #999999 3px solid;")
txtstream.WriteLine("    PADDING-RIGHT: 3px;")
txtstream.WriteLine("    PADDING-LEFT: 3px;")
txtstream.WriteLine("    FONT-WEIGHT: Bold;")
txtstream.WriteLine("    PADDING-BOTTOM: 3px;")
txtstream.WriteLine("    COLOR: white;")
txtstream.WriteLine("    PADDING-TOP: 3px;")
txtstream.WriteLine("    BORDER-BOTTOM: #999 1px solid;")
txtstream.WriteLine("    BACKGROUND-COLOR: navy;")
txtstream.WriteLine("    FONT-FAMILY: font-family: Cambria, serif;")
txtstream.WriteLine("    FONT-SIZE: 12px;")
txtstream.WriteLine("    text-align: left;")
txtstream.WriteLine("    display:table-cell;")
txtstream.WriteLine("    white-Space: nowrap='nowrap';")
txtstream.WriteLine("    width: 100%;")
txtstream.WriteLine("}")
txtstream.WriteLine("h1 {")
txtstream.WriteLine("color: antiquewhite;")
txtstream.WriteLine("text-shadow: 1px 1px 1px black;")
txtstream.WriteLine("padding: 3px;")
```

```
txtstream.WriteLine("text-align: center;")
txtstream.WriteLine("box-shadow: in2px 2px 5px rgba(0,0,0,0.5), in-2px -
2px 5px rgba(255,255,255,0.5);")
txtstream.WriteLine("}")
txtstream.WriteLine("</style>")
```

Shadow Box

```
txtstream.WriteLine("<style type='text/css'>")
txtstream.WriteLine("body")
txtstream.WriteLine("{")
txtstream.WriteLine("    PADDING-RIGHT: 0px;")
txtstream.WriteLine("    PADDING-LEFT: 0px;")
txtstream.WriteLine("    PADDING-BOTTOM: 0px;")
txtstream.WriteLine("    MARGIN: 0px;")
txtstream.WriteLine("    COLOR: #333;")
txtstream.WriteLine("    PADDING-TOP: 0px;")
txtstream.WriteLine("        FONT-FAMILY: verdana, arial, helvetica, sans-
serif;")
txtstream.WriteLine("}")
txtstream.WriteLine("table")
txtstream.WriteLine("{")
txtstream.WriteLine("    BORDER-RIGHT: #999999 1px solid;")
txtstream.WriteLine("    PADDING-RIGHT: 1px;")
txtstream.WriteLine("    PADDING-LEFT: 1px;")
txtstream.WriteLine("    PADDING-BOTTOM: 1px;")
txtstream.WriteLine("    LINE-HEIGHT: 8px;")
txtstream.WriteLine("    PADDING-TOP: 1px;")
txtstream.WriteLine("    BORDER-BOTTOM: #999 1px solid;")
txtstream.WriteLine("    BACKGROUND-COLOR: #eeeeee;")
txtstream.WriteLine("
filter:progid:DXImageTransform.Microsoft.Shadow(color='silver',    Direction=135,
Strength=16)")
```

```
txtstream.WriteLine("}")
txtstream.WriteLine("th")
txtstream.WriteLine("{")
txtstream.WriteLine("    BORDER-RIGHT: #999999 3px solid;")
txtstream.WriteLine("    PADDING-RIGHT: 6px;")
txtstream.WriteLine("    PADDING-LEFT: 6px;")
txtstream.WriteLine("    FONT-WEIGHT: Bold;")
txtstream.WriteLine("    FONT-SIZE: 14px;")
txtstream.WriteLine("    PADDING-BOTTOM: 6px;")
txtstream.WriteLine("    COLOR: darkred;")
txtstream.WriteLine("    LINE-HEIGHT: 14px;")
txtstream.WriteLine("    PADDING-TOP: 6px;")
txtstream.WriteLine("    BORDER-BOTTOM: #999 1px solid;")
txtstream.WriteLine("    BACKGROUND-COLOR: #eeeeee;")
txtstream.WriteLine("    FONT-FAMILY: font-family: Cambria, serif;")
txtstream.WriteLine("    FONT-SIZE: 12px;")
txtstream.WriteLine("    text-align: left;")
txtstream.WriteLine("    white-Space: nowrap='nowrap';")
txtstream.WriteLine("}")
txtstream.WriteLine(".th")
txtstream.WriteLine("{")
txtstream.WriteLine("    BORDER-RIGHT: #999999 2px solid;")
txtstream.WriteLine("    PADDING-RIGHT: 6px;")
txtstream.WriteLine("    PADDING-LEFT: 6px;")
txtstream.WriteLine("    FONT-WEIGHT: Bold;")
txtstream.WriteLine("    PADDING-BOTTOM: 6px;")
txtstream.WriteLine("    COLOR: black;")
txtstream.WriteLine("    PADDING-TOP: 6px;")
txtstream.WriteLine("    BORDER-BOTTOM: #999 2px solid;")
txtstream.WriteLine("    BACKGROUND-COLOR: #eeeeee;")
txtstream.WriteLine("    FONT-FAMILY: font-family: Cambria, serif;")
txtstream.WriteLine("    FONT-SIZE: 10px;")
txtstream.WriteLine("    text-align: right;")
```

```
txtstream.WriteLine("    white-Space: nowrap='nowrap';")
txtstream.WriteLine("}")
txtstream.WriteLine("td")
txtstream.WriteLine("{")
txtstream.WriteLine("    BORDER-RIGHT: #999999 3px solid;")
txtstream.WriteLine("    PADDING-RIGHT: 6px;")
txtstream.WriteLine("    PADDING-LEFT: 6px;")
txtstream.WriteLine("    FONT-WEIGHT: Normal;")
txtstream.WriteLine("    PADDING-BOTTOM: 6px;")
txtstream.WriteLine("    COLOR: navy;")
txtstream.WriteLine("    LINE-HEIGHT: 14px;")
txtstream.WriteLine("    PADDING-TOP: 6px;")
txtstream.WriteLine("    BORDER-BOTTOM: #999 1px solid;")
txtstream.WriteLine("    BACKGROUND-COLOR: #eeeeee;")
txtstream.WriteLine("    FONT-FAMILY: font-family: Cambria, serif;")
txtstream.WriteLine("    FONT-SIZE: 12px;")
txtstream.WriteLine("    text-align: left;")
txtstream.WriteLine("    white-Space: nowrap='nowrap';")
txtstream.WriteLine("}")
txtstream.WriteLine("div")
txtstream.WriteLine("{")
txtstream.WriteLine("    BORDER-RIGHT: #999999 3px solid;")
txtstream.WriteLine("    PADDING-RIGHT: 6px;")
txtstream.WriteLine("    PADDING-LEFT: 6px;")
txtstream.WriteLine("    FONT-WEIGHT: Normal;")
txtstream.WriteLine("    PADDING-BOTTOM: 6px;")
txtstream.WriteLine("    COLOR: white;")
txtstream.WriteLine("    PADDING-TOP: 6px;")
txtstream.WriteLine("    BORDER-BOTTOM: #999 1px solid;")
txtstream.WriteLine("    BACKGROUND-COLOR: navy;")
txtstream.WriteLine("    FONT-FAMILY: font-family: Cambria, serif;")
txtstream.WriteLine("    FONT-SIZE: 10px;")
txtstream.WriteLine("    text-align: left;")
```

```
txtstream.WriteLine("    white-Space: nowrap='nowrap';")
txtstream.WriteLine("}")
txtstream.WriteLine("span")
txtstream.WriteLine("{")
txtstream.WriteLine("    BORDER-RIGHT: #999999 3px solid;")
txtstream.WriteLine("    PADDING-RIGHT: 3px;")
txtstream.WriteLine("    PADDING-LEFT: 3px;")
txtstream.WriteLine("    FONT-WEIGHT: Normal;")
txtstream.WriteLine("    PADDING-BOTTOM: 3px;")
txtstream.WriteLine("    COLOR: white;")
txtstream.WriteLine("    PADDING-TOP: 3px;")
txtstream.WriteLine("    BORDER-BOTTOM: #999 1px solid;")
txtstream.WriteLine("    BACKGROUND-COLOR: navy;")
txtstream.WriteLine("    FONT-FAMILY: font-family: Cambria, serif;")
txtstream.WriteLine("    FONT-SIZE: 10px;")
txtstream.WriteLine("    text-align: left;")
txtstream.WriteLine("    white-Space: nowrap='nowrap';")
txtstream.WriteLine("    display: inline-block;")
txtstream.WriteLine("    width: 100%;")
txtstream.WriteLine("}")
txtstream.WriteLine("textarea")
txtstream.WriteLine("{")
txtstream.WriteLine("    BORDER-RIGHT: #999999 3px solid;")
txtstream.WriteLine("    PADDING-RIGHT: 3px;")
txtstream.WriteLine("    PADDING-LEFT: 3px;")
txtstream.WriteLine("    FONT-WEIGHT: Normal;")
txtstream.WriteLine("    PADDING-BOTTOM: 3px;")
txtstream.WriteLine("    COLOR: white;")
txtstream.WriteLine("    PADDING-TOP: 3px;")
txtstream.WriteLine("    BORDER-BOTTOM: #999 1px solid;")
txtstream.WriteLine("    BACKGROUND-COLOR: navy;")
txtstream.WriteLine("    FONT-FAMILY: font-family: Cambria, serif;")
txtstream.WriteLine("    FONT-SIZE: 10px;")
```

```
txtstream.WriteLine("    text-align: left;")
txtstream.WriteLine("    white-Space: nowrap='nowrap';")
txtstream.WriteLine("    width: 100%;")
txtstream.WriteLine("}")
txtstream.WriteLine("select")
txtstream.WriteLine("{")
txtstream.WriteLine("    BORDER-RIGHT: #999999 3px solid;")
txtstream.WriteLine("    PADDING-RIGHT: 6px;")
txtstream.WriteLine("    PADDING-LEFT: 6px;")
txtstream.WriteLine("    FONT-WEIGHT: Normal;")
txtstream.WriteLine("    PADDING-BOTTOM: 6px;")
txtstream.WriteLine("    COLOR: white;")
txtstream.WriteLine("    PADDING-TOP: 6px;")
txtstream.WriteLine("    BORDER-BOTTOM: #999 1px solid;")
txtstream.WriteLine("    BACKGROUND-COLOR: navy;")
txtstream.WriteLine("    FONT-FAMILY: font-family: Cambria, serif;")
txtstream.WriteLine("    FONT-SIZE: 10px;")
txtstream.WriteLine("    text-align: left;")
txtstream.WriteLine("    white-Space: nowrap='nowrap';")
txtstream.WriteLine("    width: 100%;")
txtstream.WriteLine("}")
txtstream.WriteLine("input")
txtstream.WriteLine("{")
txtstream.WriteLine("    BORDER-RIGHT: #999999 3px solid;")
txtstream.WriteLine("    PADDING-RIGHT: 3px;")
txtstream.WriteLine("    PADDING-LEFT: 3px;")
txtstream.WriteLine("    FONT-WEIGHT: Bold;")
txtstream.WriteLine("    PADDING-BOTTOM: 3px;")
txtstream.WriteLine("    COLOR: white;")
txtstream.WriteLine("    PADDING-TOP: 3px;")
txtstream.WriteLine("    BORDER-BOTTOM: #999 1px solid;")
txtstream.WriteLine("    BACKGROUND-COLOR: navy;")
txtstream.WriteLine("    FONT-FAMILY: font-family: Cambria, serif;")
```

```
txtstream.WriteLine("   FONT-SIZE: 12px;")
txtstream.WriteLine("   text-align: left;")
txtstream.WriteLine("   display: table-cell;")
txtstream.WriteLine("   white-Space: nowrap='nowrap';")
txtstream.WriteLine("   width: 100%;")
txtstream.WriteLine("}")
txtstream.WriteLine("h1 {")
txtstream.WriteLine("color: antiquewhite;")
txtstream.WriteLine("text-shadow: 1px 1px 1px black;")
txtstream.WriteLine("padding: 3px;")
txtstream.WriteLine("text-align: center;")
txtstream.WriteLine("box-shadow: in2px 2px 5px rgba(0,0,0,0.5), in-2px -
2px 5px rgba(255,255,255,0.5);")
txtstream.WriteLine("}")
txtstream.WriteLine("</style>")
```